KARTING
EXPLAINED

Graham Smith
Foreword by Paul Di Resta

THE CROWOOD PRESS

First published in 2012 by
The Crowood Press Ltd
Ramsbury, Marlborough
Wiltshire SN8 2HR

www.crowood.com

British Library Cataloguing-in-Publication Data
A catalogue record for this book is available from the British Library.

ISBN 978 1 84797 379 5

Acknowledgements
This book is dedicated to my dear wife Ann, and to my sons Nick and Malcolm and their
families. I need to thank many people for helping with the book, and although this is not an
exhaustive list, it includes Nick and Malcolm, Mark Burgess, John Davies, Paul Granger, John
Gravett, Alan Turney and Chris Walker.

All pictures by the author or kartpix.net unless otherwise credited.

Designed and typeset by Guy Croton

Printed and bound in China by Everbest Printing Co. Ltd

KARTING
E X P L A I N E D

Contents

Foreword
By Paul Di Resta

The sport of kart racing needs a book like this to explain the arts of becoming a competent driver and mechanic. When I started at age eight I was lucky to have a dad who had plenty of experience and was willing to give up many weekends in the pursuit of success. I was fortunate to be the MSA British Cadet champion in 1997 and the Junior British champion in 2001, so when I started car racing I already had nine years of competition experience. Karting is such an important nursery in which to learn how to set up a racing machine, and to learn tactics. Almost all the other drivers with me on the Formula 1 grid started their careers in kart racing.

But kart racing attracts all ages; it doesn't have to be a career step en route towards being a professional driver, engineer or team manager, although it can be all of these. For instance my brother races seriously, but as a hobby, not as a stepping stone to professional driving. I learned lots from my cousin Dario Franchitti who is now one of the most successful drivers ever in the United States, and after winning the DTM championship (German Touring Cars) I am now honoured to be a fully fledged Formula 1 driver. Please feel free to follow my career at www.pauldiresta.com.

Karting can be as low cost or expensive as you want. There are opportunities at all levels and for all ages, from occasional club racing through to high profile world championships. I can assure you there is no other discipline in motor racing that gives such fun as in kart racing. Try it – you won't be disappointed!

Photo © Sutton-images.com

Paul Di Resta currently drives for the Sahara Force India Formula 1 team.

Introduction

The sport of kart racing entertains thousands, indeed millions of people if all leisure karting is taken into account. Beware – it is addictive and very easy to become addicted to the sport, such is the buzz and adrenalin rush experienced. There are competition classes for children from the age of six to over sixty, and karts to suit almost every pocket, whilst kart racing has been the nursery for almost every Formula 1 driver. Kart racing is the cheapest form of motor sport at local club level, whilst also offering championships up to the very highest world and European level. This book will guide the reader through each step of kart racing, from how to drive safely and competitively, to gaining a competition licence, through to the first race and beyond; it also covers the basic maintenance and set-up of the kart itself.

A BRIEF HISTORY

Kart racing commenced in the USA during 1956 when an intrepid employee of the Kurtis Kraft Company called Art Ingels built up the first ever go-kart, attracting many followers – and before long bespoke racing circuits were built, too. US airmen brought the sport to the UK in 1958, and following official recognition in 1959 the popularity of the sport exploded, with over a hundred manufacturers vying for sales. This was an affordable form of four-wheeled motor sport for the working man – and still is – and luminaries such as Graham Hill and Stirling Moss were persuaded to race and demonstrate karts. In fact Stirling Moss competed in the second annual World Championships held at Nassau in the Bahamas, only ten days after winning the US Formula 1

There's nothing to beat the buzz of kart racing.

Grand Prix driver Graham Hill leading the first ever kart race held in the UK on 25 October 1959. KARTING MAGAZINE

Grand Prix. King Hussein of Jordan won a race at an English circuit, such was the enthusiasm for, and attraction of, the new sport.

Chainsaw, lawnmower and motor-cycle engines were all pressed into service; the earliest karts always had the engine or engines mounted behind the seat, but before long, engines were being specially made for karts, and were mounted alongside the seat in the same configuration as used today. A popular geared class engine was the Villiers 197cc, originally sourced from invalid carriages, and this engine type is still used today in the 210 National class by a strong band of dedicated supporters. Two-stroke non-geared engines became standardized at 100cc capacity until the late 1990s, when the trend towards more modern 125cc motors commenced. Two-stroke gearbox engines became standardized at either 125cc or 250cc, although with the near demise of two-stroke motocross, some four-stroke geared engines are appearing on the scene.

CHAMPIONSHIPS

Each local club has its own club championship, with club members enrolled automatically. Kart clubs are always eager to embrace new novice drivers, and give them plenty of assistance. The British Championships in years gone by were contested over single weekend events, but for more than twenty years have been part of a series. The major championship in the UK is the Super One Series, which commenced in 1983 and caters for all the major Cadet, Junior and Senior direct drive non-geared classes. Ten years later the predecessor to Formula Kart Stars commenced, which concentrates on Cadets and Junior classes. At an international level there are European and World Karting Championships, as well as other well supported international series.

ORGANIZATION AND GOVERNANCE

Internationally all four-wheeled motor sport is governed by the FIA – the Fédération Internationale de l'Automobile – which has its headquarters in Paris. The FIA is not just concerned with motor sport, it is also the federation of the world's leading motoring organizations. It has a particular concern for vehicle safety and the environment, whilst the associated FIA Institute has improvements in motor sport safety as its aim. Each country has a recognized club or association known as the ASN – the Automobile Sportif

Championship kart meeting paddock.

Headquarters of the Motor Sports Association.

Nationale, or National Sporting Authority – which in the UK is the Motor Sports Association (MSA).

The Motor Sports Association

The Motor Sports Council acts as the Sporting Commission, and its twenty-four members include the chairpersons of the various specialist discipline committees. It can be thought of as the motor sports parliament, while the Motor Sports Association is the civil service, administering and communicating the rules and regulations. These rules are laid down in the *Competitors and Officials Yearbook*, commonly known as the 'Blue Book'. The kart class regulations are published in the *Kart Race Yearbook*, known within the sport as the 'Gold Book'. (For further information, see Chapter 9.)

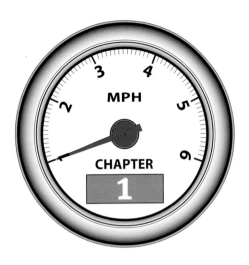

How to Get Started

Before you do anything else, visit one or more local kart circuits on their race days: talk to the officials, competitors and traders, and gather as much information as you can. Do not, however, rush out and buy a kart just yet – you may not even have to! Draw up a budget to see what you can afford: there are many options. We will concentrate here on gaining an MSA competition licence so you can race with clubs affiliated to the sport's governing body, but we will consider other options, too.

Perhaps you have tried indoor karting and enjoyed it – and if you haven't, why not try that first? Then you will probably want to go faster and further! Another route for youngsters is to participate through their schools in the British Schools Karting Championship, where teams of three drivers compete first at a local indoor circuit, before perhaps qualifying for a regional, and then a grand final. This can be a very cost-effective way of seeing if they have the aptitude for racing. There are schemes for children such as 'Let's Go Karting' or 'Racing for Buttons', where for a small fee volunteers at clubs will offer 'taster' sessions.

The scene at a typical club race.

Some clubs may have similar schemes for older drivers, so use them if you can – they are run by volunteers who will be very happy to add to your knowledge of the sport. Some schools have kart clubs under the NATSKA association – the National Association for School and Youth Group Karting in the UK. 'Arrive and drive' means that the organization supplies the race kart, and maybe even the protective clothing. Commercial outdoor circuits sometimes offer arrive-and-drive options, from low-powered four-stroke karts all the way up to fast two-strokes that approach the same performance as the karts you could own and race at MSA affiliated clubs. Some promoters even offer arrive-and-drive national championships, travelling to different circuits round the UK.

Any of these possibilities might cost less than owning your own kart, but will be fairly rigid in their options as to where and when you can race. Finally there are commer-

The MSA competition licence card.

cial circuits that offer non-MSA racing, where you still need your own kart but not a competition licence, although your competence may be tested first.

Racing at an indoor kart circuit.

Young drivers enjoying a taster session at a 'Let's Go Karting' venue.

Club 100 arrive-and-drive karts.

Former F1 World Champion Damon Hill racing in Club 100 arrive-and-drive karting.

OBTAINING A COMPETITION LICENCE

For most people the following steps are necessary in order to obtain a competition licence: purchasing the MSA go-karting starter pack, taking the novice driver test and maybe undergoing a medical examination, and finally completing the application form and sending for the licence. The MSA go-karting starter pack contains sets of the current regulations, a DVD to help prepare the applicant for the test, and the all-important novice driver licence application form.

There will be a list of places where the test can be taken: this may be at a professional Association of Racing Kart Schools (ARKS) centre, or at a participating club. In the case of the latter, a volunteer ARKS examiner will oversee the test, but unlike the official schools, they will not offer tuition. So you might be advised to attend a course at an ARKS centre, especially if you have not yet purchased a kart, and the test will be included at the end of a day's tuition.

Once your application form has been stamped with a pass, you can send off for the licence and go racing. So let us look at the test requirements in more detail.

Before the Test

The MSA go-karting starter pack can be purchased from the MSA website, or from most of the ARKS kart schools; some clubs and kart shops also keep stocks. The pack contains a wealth of information about the test, and useful advice on driving techniques. Watch the video on the DVD a few times, study the recommended parts of the regulations, and learn the meanings of all the flag signals – a 100 per cent pass rate is required on the flag knowledge section of the test. Most importantly the pack contains the first licence application form: do not lose it, as the MSA makes a hefty charge for a replacement. Each person wanting to take the test must buy a pack, but there is a small discount available for families. Depending on prior experience there can be some exemptions from taking all or part of the test (see panel).

In all cases of exemption – except possibly a foreign national with suitable experience and transferring to the United Kingdom, or drivers granted a national A level licence – the driver starts as a novice.

Exemptions to the Novice Driver Test

No pack purchase is required if the applicant holds the following:

• a race licence
• a national B licence within the previous three years
• a national A or higher licence within the previous five years
• a foreign licence, and who can prove they have the necessary experience

When applying for a kart Clubman licence no pack purchase is required, but a written test must be taken, and the applicant must:

• have proof of having held a national A kart licence or higher grade
• hold a national competitions licence from the ACU (for motorcycle racing), plus proof of competing in races at a national level in the previous three years
(In these cases a standard competition licence application form can be obtained from the MSA or their website.)

A pack purchase is required, and the applicant must take a written test, if they:

• hold a kart Clubman licence, plus have proof of finishing at least six endurance, tyro or Bambino events under MSA jurisdiction in the current or previous two years
• hold a NatSKA licence in the current or previous two years

A novice must start their racing career using black number plates with white numbers, and must start from the back of the heats until they have earned five signatures on their licence plus the ARKS novice driving test. In long-circuit racing the driver must have a yellow square with a black diagonal cross on the back of the kart.

A novice driver with black number plates.

A novice to the long circuits with a yellow cross.

A driver in a Bambino sprint competition.

Kart Clubman licence

Note that a kart Clubman licence does not require any part of the ARKS novice driver test and may even be issued on the day of the event. They can be used in endurance or tyro racing where the power of the engine is limited, or for Bambino events for six to seven-year-olds.

Endurance races are a minimum of sixty minutes in duration with a team of drivers, all over sixteen years of age. Tyro races use low power karts for entry level competition. In both cases drivers holding higher level licences are allowed to compete alongside the Clubman drivers.

Medical Requirements

All applicants for other than a kart Clubman licence aged over eighteen years are required to take a medical examination by a registered doctor. The form to be completed by the doctor is part of the licence application form. If the applicant is under eighteen, self-certification of the medical requirements is all that is required; however, when the driver applies for their first licence after reaching eighteen, a medical is required. After the age of forty-five, or when applying for an international licence, a medical is required every year. The medical can be taken before or after taking the novice driving test, but obviously before sending off the application form.

Although the form implies that the medical must be carried out by the applicant's own GP, in fact this is not strictly necessary. Sometimes at a kart or racing car show a doctor is in attendance, and will carry out the medical examinations at a lower cost than going to your GP. Usually it is best to book the examination in advance.

The MSA lists certain medical conditions that may be incompatible with the issue of a licence, such as diabetes, epilepsy, disablement of a limb, some heart conditions. If in doubt the applicant should contact the MSA's medical section administrator to see if an exemption is possible. Vision must be a minimum of 6/6 with both eyes open and spectacles if worn, and the applicant must be able to distinguish the primary colours of red and green. Competitors with asthma should wear an appropriate identity tag.

Jewellery that may prove hazardous in the event of an incident should be taken off. It is strongly recommended that competitors are immunized against tetanus.

Pre-test Practice

Before booking the test the applicant will need enough practice on a kart to show they are competent to race. If they have some prior competition driving experience this might be as little as one day; however, two or three practice days are usually necessary to reach the required performance level (see the next section). Those who have their own kart by this stage, and feel competent to drive it safely, should equip it with black number plates and white numbers to show they are a novice; on the track they should preferably set out in the company of other drivers.

Although the information in the go-karting starter pack has some useful driving tips, it would be much better for the novice applicant to take a course at a professional ARKS kart school. By so doing they will learn the correct way to drive fast and safely, and it is to be hoped will eliminate any bad habits from the outset. In the long run it could be money well spent!

The ARKS Novice Driver Test

When applying to take the ARKS novice driver test, choose either a professional ARKS kart school or an ARKS examiner at a kart club, and book up by phone. If you do not have your own kart you may need to go to an ARKS school where everything can be supplied, or the ARKS examiner may be able to suggest a local kart shop from where you might hire a kart for the test. Either way the hire of the kart will cost extra, over and above the test fee. Some schools only offer the test as part of a day's tuition package, while some clubs offer incentives such as a voucher towards membership, or the entry fee for your first race. Check them all out and make your choice.

On arrival at the agreed time the applicant will need to sign on and pay; if under eighteen years of age, a parent or guardian must also be present and counter sign. It may be necessary to sign on and pay the practice fee to the

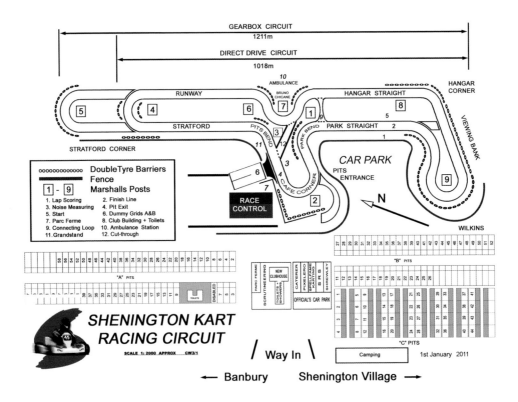

A track diagram showing the marshal posts.

circuit separately. You should then watch the DVD that is in the pack together with the instructor or examiner, so they can explain anything that is unclear, and elaborate on what might be asked in the test questionnaire. You should, of course, have viewed the DVD several times before coming for the test, remembering that all the answers to the questions will be explained in the video. The instructor should also familiarize you with the track layout, highlighting the entrance and exit, and the marshal post positions. They should cover any higher risk areas, and should explain what to do if the kart spins or breaks down. They will be happy to answer questions at any time.

The test consists of two parts, the written test and the driving test, and they can be taken in either order. The instructor will ask for the applicant's licence application form, and even if you have not taken the medical, he will want to see that the form has been signed, confirming there are no medical issues, and may even check your colour vision by asking you to distinguish different coloured flags. Remember that the instructor is not qualified to decide whether any medical issues will prevent the issue of a licence – only the MSA can decide this, so passing the test is not a guarantee that the licence will be issued.

The instructor will take down all the applicant's personal details, including name, address, date of birth and licence application form number to enter on the test sheets – and of course you need to pay for the test. The test fee includes VAT at the current rate, and a cheque is usually preferred.

The Driving Test

Whether you are using your own kart, or a kart you have hired for the day, the instructor will want to ensure that it complies with general MSA safety regulations, and is approximately at the correct class weight. Then kart and driver – complete with race suit and helmet – are weighed together; if they are under the designated weight for the class of kart, ballast is added, usually in the form of lead blocks.

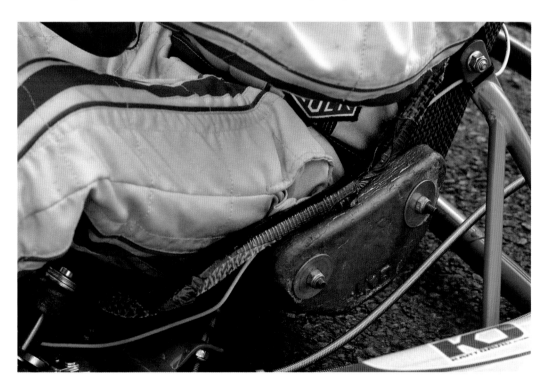

Lead ballast used to bring the kart and driver above the minimum class weight.

Then the examiner or instructor will probably invite you to familiarize yourself with the kart, the circuit and the track conditions of the day. They will watch, and may give some general tips and advice. They will also set a target time for the conditions on the day, and the type of kart used. This target time is 10 per cent slower than a mid-grid time for the class, and is designed to show that the novice racer is quick enough not to be lapped in a heat. On a later session they will record your lap times, and make an assessment on the various categories as to whether you pass or fail.

The test is to see if the driver is capable of racing, and to ensure that his driving is good enough so as not to put other drivers at risk. It is not a requirement to drive perfectly, but you must be safe, competent and faster than the target time. The examiner or instructor will complete the remarks section on his form, and whether you pass or fail, will pass on any recommendations and explain how to correct any errors.

The Written Test

In the written test the applicant will be given the questionnaire and asked to tick the answer they believe to be correct. There are five possible answers to each question, and all the flag questions must be answered correctly, plus at least eight out of the other ten questions. Three of these are on safety, the remainder are general. Remember there could be a group taking the test at the same time. If a minor needs help with reading or understanding the questions, the questions and answers may be read out, leaving the candidate to make the choice. Ten minutes should be given for this part, and of course the applicant is not allowed to refer to the regulations. All the questions are covered in the video on the DVD, so make sure you have viewed it thoroughly.

The Flag Signals

The MSA 'Blue Book' describes the meaning of the different flags used in motor racing and kart racing; this information can be found in the circuit racing section. Note that there are two flags used only for kart racing: the yellow/black quartered flag and the green with yellow chevron false start flag.

FACT

Driving Test Parameters

The following parameters are required to pass the novice driving test:

• Correct hand positions on the steering wheel
• Smooth turn-in
• Apex point
• Corner entry and exit
• Contact with kerbs
• Correct use of the throttle
• Sufficient braking before corners
• Smooth braking
• Awareness in traffic
• Safe entry and exit to track
• Synchronization of throttle and brake
• General co-ordination
• Correct racing lines
• Driving to instruction

And for gearbox karts the applicant will also be assessed on:
• Correct use of the clutch
• Correct use and synchronization of the gears

The De-Brief

After the test there should be a de-brief. Don't be too disappointed if you fail either of the tests, there is always the chance to take them again at a future date, and they are separately priced. The instructor has the final say on a pass or fail, so even if you think you have passed the sections, if your attitude is felt to be incompatible with safe racing, or if the instructor feels you do not really understand the rules, they could still fail you. The instructor should go over any weak points with you, and help you to choose an appropriate class if you are still undecided. They will stamp your licence application form if you have passed, so you can send it off to the MSA for the licence.

A licence runs from 1 January to 31 December each year, so if you take the test near the year end it might make sense to apply for the following year's licence. If you have only passed one part, you will be given a pass slip for that part only. If you are under eighteen years of age and do not need a medical examination, you are permitted to use the licence application form in place of a licence; thus you can take it to the signing on with any fee needed for the licence, and the competition secrctary will check with the MSA steward to ensure you are permitted to race. The competition secretary will keep your form and send it off to the MSA after the event. You are only allowed to do this once. It is also important to get a signature for that first event by submitting the white card that is bound into the 'Blue Book', to the competition secretary at signing on.

Sending for the Licence

Normally the applicant will ensure they have a completed licence application form stamped with the novice driver test pass, the medical examination completed if applicable,

RIGHT: *An ARKS examiner overseeing the driving test.*

BELOW: *Taking the written test.*

together with an identity photograph and any fee; they will then send it off to the MSA. There is a fast track option at extra cost, but if the application is outside the busy Christmas and New Year renewal period, the return time is usually just over a week. It is possible to track its progress on the MSA website, and you should receive an email acknowledgement.

CHOOSING A CLASS

Although at first glance there seem to be a lot of classes to choose from, in practice these can be narrowed down quite dramatically. First of all, go to your local kart circuits to see what is popular, because there is no point buying into a class that is not raced, or rarely raced, at your local club. Next, take into account your age, weight and height: kart classes always have a minimum combined weight for kart and driver, so small drivers do not have a performance advantage over bigger drivers, but the class weight cannot cater for very large drivers of that age group. If it did, then the small drivers would have to carry a massive and potentially unsafe amount of ballast, usually in the form of lead blocks, although sometimes more exotic materials such as tungsten are used. Usually the practical upper limit is 20kg.

At some point therefore a large driver will be above the class weight, and potentially less competitive against those who are only just above the class weight limit. There are classes for heavier drivers, such as the Rotax Max 177, and where classes have plenty of power such as the gearbox categories, excess driver weight may not make such a difference.

Bambino Classes

Children as young as six years of age can enjoy karting in the Bambino class. However, these young drivers can only take part in competition after they have followed a carefully graduated training programme, overseen by an ARKS instructor or examiner – although at the time of writing no ARKS novice driver test is required. The karts are smaller than Cadets, and the maximum speed is about 60km/h or maybe less.

Not all clubs will offer this class, primarily due to time constraints during their meetings, but there are plenty of places where such young contestants can practise safely. Signatures gained in competition count towards an exemption from the ARKS driving test.

Cadet Classes

At eight years old a youngster can race a Cadet kart – small minikarts that reach a top speed of about 80km/h. Cadet classes are for eight- to thirteen-year-olds.

At the time of writing there are two engine types to consider: Honda and Comer, both started by a pull cord. However, in 2013 a new engine for this age category is planned. Although youngsters can stay in the class until the end of the year of their thirteenth birthday, most will move up before that as they become too heavy and uncompetitive for the class.

The Honda engine is a GX160 mass-produced, adapted industrial engine, so it could be said to be 'cheap and cheerful'. The owner can carry out all servicing and rebuilds if they wish. Being a four-stroke it runs on normal petrol, and its life between rebuilds is considerable – and it needs no more than a precautionary oil change between meetings. Its only disadvantage is that the engine is heavier than the equivalent two-strokes, and a driver can grow too big for this class earlier than in the two-stroke equivalent.

The Comer W60 is a two-stroke engine, so requires racing oil mixing in with the petrol. All engines are sourced through one UK importer, and are sealed so that only authorized agents can carry out any major rebuild. The basic engine is more expensive than the Honda, and requires more regular routine servicing. It, too, is based on an industrial engine, so tolerances can vary slightly between engines; therefore at the higher levels of the sport, competitors or engine tuners select parts and engines to optimize these tolerances while still meeting the tightly written regulations, potentially putting up the cost of owning a championship-winning engine.

At the time of writing this book, both categories have their own national championships, although the Comer Cadet is used for the MSA British Championship; however, that may change in the future. Some clubs have only Honda Cadets racing, others only Comer Cadets, and some a mixture. So the same advice applies: go to your local club and see what is popular, and also take into account your budget. Tyres in Cadets are less stressed due to the low power, so tend to last for several races, perhaps even a season.

Youngsters can start racing Cadets at the age of eight; this is the Comer variety.

A Honda Cadet, which uses an economical four-stroke engine.

The Super Cadet Class

The Super Cadet class was introduced in 2011 as an intermediate class between the Cadet and Junior classes, for eleven- to fourteen-year-olds. The Super Cadet uses a 60cc two-stroke engine giving out about 10bhp, and has an electric self starter. Although the MSA may decide in the future to restrict the competition class to only one engine, there are currently several Super Cadet engines to choose from, and they are not sealed so competitors can do their own rebuilds and tuning within the limits of the regulations.

The engines are bespoke kart engines manufactured to very fine tolerances, and so are more likely to be very similar in performance 'out of the box' – however, they are consequently more expensive than mass-produced engines. This may not be a class to start in as a novice.

Super Cadets for ten to fourteen-year-olds.

Junior Classes and Senior Equivalents

Drivers can start in most of the junior classes at the age of eleven, or age thirteen for the more powerful categories, and can remain in the class until the end of the year of their seventeenth birthday, with one or two exceptions. There are minimum weight limitations and sometimes a minimum height, designed to prevent drivers who are too small having to carry excessive ballast, or being too small to handle the size of kart. There are three main categories to choose from: Rotax, TKM and Blue, plus a number of niche classes, including some four-stroke categories.

The MiniMax, the lower power Junior kart from the Rotax family.

The Rotax Categories

The Rotax categories are currently the most popular classes in the UK. Drivers can start in MiniMax at age eleven, transfer into Junior Max at age thirteen, or the year of their thirteenth birthday with prior experience, and then into Senior Max at age sixteen, or in the year of their sixteenth birthday with prior experience. Drivers must leave MiniMax by the end of the year of their fifteenth birthday.

The engine is a modern water-cooled 125cc two-stroke, with electric starter, usually called TAG, standing for 'touch and go'. The engines are sealed so only authorized agents can undertake major rebuilds; however, they can be used for longer periods between rebuilds than many other classes. The same basic engine is used for all the age categories, but only the Senior category has a power valve; even so, it is not always worth converting from a Junior engine to a Senior engine.

The MiniMax engine is the same as the Junior Max engine, but fitted with an exhaust restrictor to cut down the power to an appropriate level. The Rotax categories might be a little more expensive to purchase than the simplest kart engine types, but have a longer life between rebuilds.

There is a category for drivers weighing over 85kg which is raced at some clubs.

The Junior Max is one of the most powerful Junior categories.

TAG karts have an electric start button.

Senior Rotax engines have a power valve.

Rotex Max Senior class racing.

The TKM Category

The TKM two-stroke categories of Junior TKM and TKM Extreme have traditional air-cooled engines of 100cc and 115cc respectively. Although there are clutch and TAG engine options in their simplest and cheapest form, the kart has to be picked up at the back and pushed to start. To stop at the end of a practice session or race, the brake is applied until the engine stalls.

The engines are not sealed, so many competitors carry out their own maintenance and rebuilds, which are required more often than in the modern water-cooled classes. Rotax has supplanted TKM as the most popular category, so not all clubs offer it at all, but it is a very economical class to race in and there are a number of different weight categories with different sized restrictors to equalize performance.

The company that makes the engines, Tal-Ko, also offers a four-stroke long-life engine; it is sealed, however, so only Tal-Ko can carry out any rebuilds required.

Push-starting a traditional direct-drive kart with no clutch.

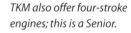

TKM also offer four-stroke engines; this is a Senior.

Formula Blue Category

The Formula Blue category also offers a range of weights for drivers of different sizes, with different sized restrictors to equalize performance in both Junior and Senior categories. The engines are water-cooled and TAG, meaning they have an electric starter, and are 100cc two-strokes with a slightly larger option. They are all sourced through a company called TABOR, who controls the regulations for the class, subject to MSA approval. They are not raced universally so check if they are offered at your local club.

Formula Blue is an alternative to Rotax raced at some clubs; this is the Junior variety.

Easykarts race only in their own championship; this is a Junior, but there are Senior and Cadet categories as well.

Easykart

Easykart is a commercial championship series with classes for all age categories. Although the driver needs an MSA competition licence, the karts are only raced at the Easykart club championship series. The cost of the kart, which is normally owned by the driver but may sometimes be hired for the events, is perhaps more economical than other classes. Add-ons and adjustments are very limited and tightly controlled.

Club 100

Club 100 is one of a number of the so-called 'arrive and drive' series where all the equipment is supplied by the promoters. There are categories for senior, heavy and light drivers, and of course there is no need to transport a kart to the race circuit. No MSA competition licence is needed, but the promoters will require previous practice or evidence of competence in kart racing.

International Classes

As well as the popular national classes, there are inter-national classes – such as KF3 for juniors and KF2 for seniors – which are raced as major championships both in the UK and abroad. The regulations for these are made by the international governing body, the CIK, and only minimal changes are made for UK racing. Some clubs may offer these classes for major race meetings, or prior to a visit by a national championship so drivers can have some race practice at the particular track. Both use a modern, 125cc water-cooled TAG engine, quite highly tuned but with maximum rev limits. They are not classes to start off in.

Rotax categories are also raced all across the world, and offer a Grand Final for the best drivers from each country each year, as well as a European championship and various other one-off events. Formula KGP is another type of category which is raced in a number of countries as well as having been introduced to the UK. It also has an annual championship event, and the category is promoted by the Birel manufacturer and importer.

The engines are all made by BMB, Birel's engine manufacturing arm, and any chassis conforming to MSA regulations is permitted. The engine is not sealed, so driver maintenance is possible and some limited tuning is allowed. There are some other niche categories of a similar nature.

KF3 is the premier international Junior category.

Formula KGP (for seniors) is a relative newcomer and offers performance somewhere between Rotax and KF2.

Four-stroke categories

'Prokart' is the term used for four-stroke powered karts, usually the Honda GX160 as in Honda Senior and Junior. Although there are sprint races, many of these types of kart are used in endurance races, which last anything from one hour to twenty-four using a team of drivers. This can cut down the cost, as the kart is shared between a number of people. Races are offered for both MSA licence holders and for those who do not have a competition licence.

There are other low-powered four-stroke categories such as World Formula, and some for a variety of higher-powered four-stroke engines, usually of 250cc. There are even some rotary engines, which are very compact and can produce amazing amounts of power, however none of these is currently approved for MSA racing.

Honda Senior prokarting offers exceptionally economical racing.

Gearbox Classes

An alternative to consider for senior drivers is one of the gearbox categories, or 'shifter karts' as they are referred to in other countries. There are 125cc six-speed and 250cc five- and six-speed classes. By 'six speed' we mean they have six gears so the engine can be kept at its optimum power output rev range all the time. The gears are sequentially changed, in a way similar to a motor cycle but with a gear lever next to the steering wheel. The clutch is normally only needed for the standing start or when recovering from a spin, and may be either hand- or foot-operated. KZ2, or ICC UK as it is sometimes known in the UK, is the category for 125cc engines, or KZ1 for the top international races.

The 250 National uses 250cc two-stroke single-cylinder motocross engines, but these have to be sourced from older motorcycles because the major motorcycle companies no longer make production two-stroke engines. The Superkart 250cc engines have twin cylinders and are mostly used on the long motor-racing circuits, achieving up to 240km/h. Most use derivations of the 1980s' design of an in-line twin cylinder from Rotax.

KZ2 is the name for six-speed gearbox 125cc karts.

A 250 National kart can reach 100mph on short-circuit tracks, and 130mph on long circuits.

Very high performance Superkarts race on the long motor-racing tracks, and can reach speeds of 150mph.

The Superkarts offer the same sort of performance as many single-seater racing categories, whilst a surprising number of Indycar and Formula 1 drivers practice in KZ2, believing it is the nearest practical alternative to their usual car to keep sharp and fit. Most, but not all circuits accept gearbox karts.

Historic and Classic Karts

One other cost-effective option is to find and perhaps restore a historic or classic kart. There is a thriving British Historic Kart Club that organizes demonstrations at major meetings all over the country, has links with overseas events, and has a non-MSA racing series as well. Generally the cut-off date if a kart is to be considered as a classic is 1982, and historic karts start from 1956.

Electric Karts

Electric karts may become more popular in the future, but at the time of writing no categories have been approved for MSA racing. They do offer potentially huge amounts of torque and therefore amazing acceleration.

ACQUIRING A KART

Once a decision has been made as to the best class to start in, the next decision is whether to buy or hire a kart, to employ the help of a team, or go it alone.

Doing it Yourself

Some planning is required before buying and keeping a racing kart. First of all, somewhere secure is needed, to store the kart and carry out maintenance, usually a garage or shed. A means of transport to the race track will also be needed, usually a trailer or small van, although a kart can be fitted into an estate car or hatch-back of reasonable size if the wheels and bodywork are first removed, and if the engine and bodywork are removed, it is possible to use a roof rack.

Now for the optional parts! Most drivers will find life easier with a helper, at the least someone who can help lift the kart on or off the trolley or stand – although trolleys can be found that are designed to lift a kart in a one-person operation. If the kart needs pushing to start, then again a helper is a necessity. The next option is to have an awning or easy-up to protect the driver, mechanic and kart from the worst of the weather whilst fettling the kart between races.

All sorts of small trailers are used to transport karts and spares.

Small easy-up awnings are popular.

What to Buy, Used or New?

The decision as to whether to buy a new or a second-hand kart will most likely be dictated by the size of the budget available, but certainly for a driver's first season it is worth considering a used machine because not so much is lost if a different make of kart or class is thought to be better once they are more experienced. Another possibility is to buy a new engine and put it on a used kart – then the history of the engine is known from the outset. Since a new driver needs quite a lot of ancillary equipment, buying used can have its advantages; for example, if the seller is moving class or leaving the sport there may be a job lot of the trolley, wet weather tyres, spares and perhaps even a race suit on offer.

More details on checking over a kart are given in Chapter 3, but basically if buying second-hand, ensure the kart is clean and straight. 'Clean' means not too many scrapes underneath, tidy bodywork and no welded up breakages. Checking a kart for straightness is easy: use a measuring tape to ensure that the distance from a point on the front axle to the middle of the rear axle is within 2–3mm, and if possible also check diagonally underneath. Karts often take on a 'set', where one front corner sits higher than the other, but this is relatively easy to correct by putting the low corner on a stand and bouncing on the high side whilst some heavy helpers hold the rear end firm. Again, refer to Chapter 3 for more details.

Usually it is best to see the engine running, either on the stand or by having a test drive at a race circuit. If engine is sealed, then check that the number on the seal matches the number in the log book, which should show all the service history.

If the engine is not sealed it is quite common to ask to take the cylinder head and perhaps the cylinder off to make an internal inspection. Perhaps recent receipts of spares or rebuilds can be shown. Unless a scrutineer is

Before purchase, inspect a kart from side to side and diagonally for straightness.

Sealed engines will come with a logbook.

willing to check the engine for eligibility there is always a risk that the engine may not be legal to race, but purchasing from a well known trader may provide more come-back than a private sale.

If the budget stretches to buying a new kart, then there is a balance to be drawn between the best price, and the dealer that can offer the best local service. Look to see which karts are popular, and which are at the winning end of the race results in the class chosen. Once more experience has been gained there is always the option to go against the crowd, but not to begin with.

Racing with a Team

Racing with a team may appear to be more expensive in the short term, but could be cheaper in the long term as the team's experience may help you avoid making expensive mistakes. Teams can offer several options: from a full blown arrive-and-drive, where the competitor just needs to turn up with his or her race wear and licence and hire everything else from the team; to a middle way, which is for the competitor to own the kart but have the team maintain it; to the cheapest option, which is to pay for space in the team awning, perhaps sharing a mechanic, but bringing the kart to the meeting oneself.

Teams will have the expertise and data bank to put the appropriate settings on the kart to suit the prevailing weather and track conditions. They will have more tools and equipment, from set-up gauges to tyre removers to air compressors, and in an emergency can throw more man-power at a kart for repairs, or for changes from dry to wet weather settings. The smaller local teams are probably a good place to start, then when the competitor wants to move on to national level championships the bigger teams can be considered.

CLUB CHOICE

The next decision will be which club to join. Most likely the obvious choice will be the nearest club, but there may be other considerations. Perhaps the club only caters for four-stroke kart racing, whilst the desired class is two-stroke – or vice versa – or perhaps the club operates on a day of the month that doesn't suit you. Most clubs have a fixed Sunday in the month for racing, with practice the day before, so it is quite possible to race at one club on the first Sunday of the month, and at another on, say, the third Sunday, and thus have two races each month.

Clubs usually offer discounts on race and practice fees to club members, and normally a driver is automatically enrolled into the club championship once a member. A competitor will need to join at least one club, and most are members of the Association of British Kart Clubs, so the members of these clubs are invited to race as guests at neighbouring clubs. The decision to join more than one club will be made because you wish to be part of that club championship, or to take advantage of the discounts. Visit the clubs and chat to the officials: generally they will all be friendly and helpful to newcomers.

THE ROLE OF MECHANICS AND PARENTS

The term 'mechanic' can cover a whole range of activities, from the basic help required to put a kart on the grid for a race, through tuning the kart to the track conditions, to interpreting data collected from on-board loggers. The basic duties, sometimes entrusted to a spouse, partner or friend, are to help take the kart out of the van or trailer and fit the wheels, fill it with fuel, and push the trolley to the grid for a race. Once set down on the ground, the mechanic will take the trolley to the trolley park to await the kart's return, stand by the kart whilst it is started (or push it to start), and perhaps take lap times during the race or practice. He will be able to run and fetch a set of different tyres should the weather suddenly change. He will also help recover the kart from the track should it break down or be involved in an incident – it is to be hoped an infrequent occurrence.

Experienced mechanics will observe the kart's behaviour on the track and make recommendations or decisions as to how best to optimise the settings for the next session. They will also act as a driver coach, suggesting ways to go round the track faster, or better strategies for the race. Good mechanics can change an axle or an engine in an amazingly short period of time, and most will be able to download data from on-board data-loggers and make basic interpretations – but the

A typical kart circuit: this is Rowrah in the Lake District.

best will be experts in the field and will use the data to help optimise the kart set-up. Some mechanics will be ex-drivers – some even up to World Champion level are available for hire. They will be more than just a mechanic and driver coach, but will be a mentor as well.

A parent can be all of the above, but in addition has the child's welfare to consider. Either the parent or guardian, or the team, may need an entrant's licence, and if responsibility for a minor under eighteen years of age is handed over to a team manager, the club may need to see a letter of agreement. If school is being missed, a letter giving permission from the school may also be required. The parent may be employing a mechanic to look after the kart, but must still ensure the youngster is eating, drinking and behaving appropriately. This is espe-cially important at the end of the race or practice day, when children may be left to their own devices at the circuit. Parents need to be aware of what they are up to.

The benefit of sport, and kart racing in particular, as an aid to family bonding cannot be underestimated. Once a family is dedicated to the sport, it can become all-

consuming – but however much or little time is devoted to it, kart racing offers a great opportunity for parents and children to work together in harmony.

Whoever countersigns a minor's entry or practice is responsible for that child, and must accompany them to any hearing or investigation by an official, usually the clerk of the course or the MSA steward.

Psychological Support

An important part of the role of a mechanic or parent is first to help the driver prepare for a race, and to support them after a setback. Make sure the kart is prepared for the race or practice session in good time to get to the grid area, so there is no last-minute panic; at a practice session this also makes it easier to pick one's spot for starting: maybe the driver wants to start at the front and run with the quicker drivers, or perhaps they want to be right at the back, to be on their own, or to better test something without the distraction of other karts passing. The mechanic should ensure the driver has their helmet

All hands on deck to help with an axle change.

and gloves to hand, and be on the grid in good time for the engine start.

A few words of encouragement before the driver goes on to the track are always good, along with a quick reminder of the objectives of the session.

There is always something positive to be learned from a test session or race, even if it is only to prove that a certain direction in set-up has not worked out. The mechanic should also be timing a rival driver, one known to be a consistent front runner, so comparisons can be made. But it is also important that he looks at the rival's set-up, to see if they are using new or worn tyres for instance, and takes that into account. The support person should always talk up the positive aspects, then mention

Mechanic offers some words of advice pre-race.

the down side of the session, but be sure to finish the debrief on a positive note again, looking forward to the next session and what can be done to improve.

Coping with a Setback

Everyone has a setback at some time. Perhaps a first corner incident has relegated the driver to trawling round at the back in the vain hope of catching the pack, or maybe the kart just isn't working well and the driver is gradually falling back. Whatever the cause, they are likely to come in angry and disappointed, and the first action of the mechanic or parent must be to calm them down, be solicitous and look for positives.

CHAPTER
2

Health and Safety

SAFETY IN THE SPORT

Look at the signs pinned round a kart- or motor-racing circuit: they say 'Warning – motor racing can be dangerous' – not '*is* dangerous' but '*can be*'. Everyone must therefore take the utmost care to minimize risks, and this starts with the use of the correct approved safety apparel. Minimizing risk also means wearing ear protection in noisy environments, and having a fire extinguisher to hand in the pit area. It means tying up long hair and ensuring it is tucked in safely, and not wearing loose clothing such as scarves or hoodies. The kart itself must also be checked over carefully, and be fitted with all the correct safety equipment (*see* Chapter 4).

RACEWEAR

There are strict rules concerning racewear, which form part of the ARKS novice driver test. The regulations are contained in the competitor safety and karting sections of the MSA's *Competitor and Officials Yearbook*. Circuits not running under the MSA authority may have slightly different rules.

Helmets

Be very careful when choosing a helmet that it accords with the regulations, and be aware that there are helmets for all motor sport, helmets that are just allowed for kart racing, and special helmets for children. Generally

A driver in suit and helmet.

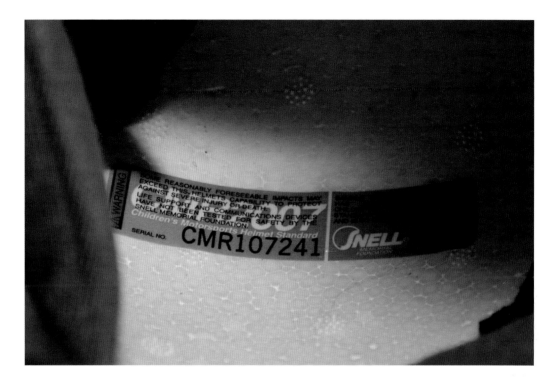

The Snell CMR label inside a youth helmet.

FACT

Crash helmet standards accepted for motor sport

• FIA 8860 – 2004 (used in the higher formulae)
• Snell SA2010
• Snell SA2005
• Snell SA2000 (may be withdrawn on 01.01.15)
• SFI Foundation 31.1a, 31.2a
• BS 6658 Type A/FR (red label – may be withdrawn on 01.01.16)
• Kart Only
• Snell K98, K2005, K2010
• CMR & CMS2007 (mandatory for all under-fifteens in international kart racing, all Cadets and Bambinos in national racing in the UK, and from 01.01.13 all under-fifteens racing in the UK)
Note: In general the Snell standards are permitted for a period of ten years from the start date of the standard, but may be longer. Examples of the labels for the different standards can be found in the MSA *Competitors Yearbook*.

speaking, helmets that are legal for motor-cycle road use will not be accepted in motor-racing or kart racing, so a specialist supplier and not a motor-cycle shop needs to be contacted. Motor-cycle helmets are often mass-production items tested to the ECE R22-05 standard, and may therefore not accord with the very strict motor-racing standards: so do not purchase a ECE 22-05 helmet. The helmets for kart racing only are tested to the same standard as all motor-racing helmets, but just don't have the fire-proofing so can be slightly cheaper.

The FIA Institute for Motor Sport Safety and Sustainability developed a new standard for helmets specially designed to fit youths aged from seven to eighteen. These helmets are very light, and shaped especially for a child's head. An adult full-face helmet may sit on the shoulders of a child before the crown is in contact with the top of the child's head.

The most common standards for crash helmets come from the USA's Snell Memorial Foundation, although there are several others accepted. Helmets to a British standard may still be accepted, but are being phased out.

Choosing a Helmet

The first thing to say is that you have only one head, so purchase the best helmet you can afford. If possible go to a specialist motor-sport store or kart shop, and try on helmets for size and comfort.

A helmet should be a tight fit, squeezing the cheek bones to some extent, as inevitably the padding will compact in use. Rock the helmet from side to side and front to back with the strap done up, to ensure it remains firmly fitted at all angles with no or minimal movement. If given the choice between a narrow aperture formula car-type helmet, or a more open aperture motor cycle-type helmet, the latter may offer more visibility and be better for peripheral vision. Wear it for a few minutes to ensure continued comfort before deciding. Check the weight: the lighter the better. The new CMR/CMS standards for youths are exceedingly light, putting less strain on the neck.

Helmets from different manufacturers with ostensibly the same size marking may actually be a slightly different fit, so always try before you buy. Sizes are usually from XS

The green MSA approval sticker shows that this helmet is for karting only.

('Extra Small', or approximately 52–54cm measured around the circumference of the head from the forehead and just above the ears) to XXL for 'Extra Large' (63–64cm); for young drivers an XXS size may be available.

Find out if replacement visors are easily obtained, and if they can be purchased in a darker tinted colour for use in bright sunshine. Although an open-face helmet worn with goggles may technically still be permitted, always go for a full-face helmet. Look for a helmet that has some venting, designed to help prevent it misting up; often the vents are adjustable and can be opened or closed, to aid cooling. Try the helmet with a balaclava if you plan to wear one. High end helmets may come with external fittings for HANS devices, used in cars to prevent excessive movement of the head and neck in an impact, but these are not used in kart racing.

A helmet should be replaced every few years, irrespective of damage. A few light scratches may be acceptable, but if a scratch reaches the gel coating or there is crazing on the surface, then it might well be rejected by the event scrutineers. If a helmet is dropped on to a hard surface, then it may be damaged and should be replaced; keep the helmet in a soft padded bag for protection when it is not in use. Stickers may cause damage to the integrity of the shell, so should be avoided. If the helmet must be painted, go to a reputable company because certain paints may also attack certain types of helmet shell. Remember that paint adds weight, potentially increasing neck strain.

At or before the first MSA race meeting the helmet will have to be inspected by a safety scrutineer, and an MSA sticker attached to the right-hand side where it can easily be seen. This service costs a couple of pounds. Different coloured stickers are used: green for a kart-only helmet, yellow for the CMR/CMS youth helmets, and blue for the general motor-sport helmet.

The stickers may be serial numbered so they can be traced back to the official who purchased them from the MSA, and a sticker may be removed by a scrutineer if he suspects damage, or that the helmet is no longer eligible for racing. There is some very useful advice about caring for helmets in the competitor safety section of the MSA *Competitors and Officials Year Book*.

Race Suits

Race suits for kart racing are very different from race suits used in race cars and rally cars. For cars, the primary protection is against fire, but in kart racing it is against abrasion on the track surface should the driver be ejected, so leather suits with a minimum thickness of 1.2mm must be worn on the higher speed, long circuit races, and on short circuit races suits must be homologated (approved and registered) by the CIK and FIA (the world governing bodies for kart and car racing). A list of currently homologated suits is available on the CIK website, and the homologation registration number is shown by embroidery on the collar of the suit.

The homologation label on a race suit.

Selection of race suits in a shop.

The registration number will include a year code, which might be the year the suit was homologated, or the year that the homologation expired, meaning that it cannot be sold new after that date. So far the MSA accepts all suits homologated under the auspices of the FIA from 1998, but for international racing only a current homologation may be acceptable. Sample labels are shown in the karting section of the MSA *Competitors and Officials Yearbook*. In the future, the MSA may decide to exclude the use of older suits.

There are two grades of suit: Level 1, which may only be used for national level racing, and a higher specification Level 2 which is mandatory for international competition. To provide the necessary abrasion resistance, suits are made from a variety of proprietary fabrics. Some may have a lining to absorb sweat and moisture.

A good comfortable fit is essential, leaving plenty of room for movement to operate the controls of the kart. Sit down on the floor and bend your knees to make sure the legs are sufficiently long so they do not ride up over the ankles when racing. You may want to make sure that there is room to wear a rib protector, which could become a mandatory item in the future. Race suits can be made to measure for a small extra fee. Colour is a matter of personal preference, but embroidery or patches can also be added later.

A selection of race boots.

Gloves and Boots

There are no specific standards in kart racing for either **gloves** or **boots**. The current regulations for gloves state that they must be complete, not mitts, and with no open backs to them. For boots, the only current regulation is that they must cover and protect the driver's ankles. However, most drivers will use gloves and boots that are especially made for racing purposes. They should always of course be a comfortable fit, and allow for an overlap of the race-suit.

Optional Racewear

When it is wet, it is all but essential to wear an **all-in-one wet suit** to cover and protect the race suit. Some are transparent so that sponsors' logos can still be viewed or seen in photographs or video. Some drivers use large-size latex or vinyl gloves over their race gloves to keep these dry; similarly rubber over-boots can be worn over race boots. There is also a product called a **whirly visor**, which is strapped on over the regular helmet visor and throws the raindrops to one side as it spins, turned by the forward motion. The visor is not seen so often these days, however, and good anti-fog and rain-dispersant applications are more commonly applied to the helmet visor.

Many drivers wear **rib protectors**, and the FIA Safety Institute is investigating drawing up an approved standard for these products. Some clubs and some countries recommend the use of **neck braces** for youngsters, but the jury is still out on these products. It is important that if one is worn, it does not push the helmet above the crown of the head.

Ear plugs should be considered a necessity, unless the kart engine is particularly quiet. Long-term exposure to noise can lead to hearing loss, or tinnitus, and once that happens it is usually too late to make it better. Tinnitus is the term for hearing noises even though there are actually no external sounds. Noise is generated by the wind rushing past the driver as well as the more obvious engine noise. Ear plugs can be obtained that reduce the noise without totally eliminating it, so for instance a kart coming up behind to overtake could still be heard.

A driver wearing a whirly visor for better visibility in the wet.

SUSTENANCE – FOOD AND DRINK

Eating and drinking sensibly will pay dividends on race weekends. It is best not to eat up to an hour before a race, but drink plenty of liquids. Avoid taking drinks containing caffeine or too much sugar – the quick boost they will give won't last, and is best left for after the last race, before prize giving.

It's best to bring your own food to the race track, as you can never guarantee being able to buy the right kind at the local burger van. Pasta and fruit is good: food that gives energy but is light is best.

FITNESS

Clearly you have to be fairly fit to race a kart competitively. Cardio and upper body strength are probably the areas to concentrate on. The best plan is to go to your local gym and get onto a training schedule. Jogging, swimming and cycling are all good for general fitness, and press-ups are good for building muscle tone in your arms and shoulders. Even so, there is nothing to beat seat time in the kart.

Before and After a Race

It is a good idea to warm up before a race by jogging on the spot, or even skipping, and doing some stretches.

Stretching prior to a race.

A fire extinguisher for every competitor is mandatory.

Stretch the upper back, the quads and the hamstrings as a minimum. Do the stretches again after the race, just like you would do before and after a jogging run or any other form of exercise.

MENTAL PREPARATION

Visualization is a technique used by all top drivers. Close your eyes and mentally drive round the track, paying particular attention to braking points, turn-in points, and if it is a geared kart, the gear changes. The best drivers can start a watch at the beginning of a 'mental' lap, then when it ends, will find that their virtual time is within a few tenths of an actual race time. Memorize the numbers of the drivers next to you, and in front of and behind you on the starting grid, then close your eyes and think of the various scenarios that could play out at the start, and how you would react. Decide on a goal for the starting phase of the race and visualize how you would reach that goal.

SAFETY IN THE PITS

Be very aware of minimizing risk in the awning, pit or paddock area. Having a good first-aid kit to hand is essential.

Fire might be the most serious potential risk, so fire extinguishers are a must. The mandate of the Association of British Kart Clubs is a minimum of one extinguisher to BSEN3 standard of minimum size 55B per driver, but in practice a more sensible size is a 70B or larger. If an enclosed awning is being used, then the ABKC recommends having a 2kg foam extinguisher at the entrance, and if the awning is being used by more than one driver, then two of them.

A business enterprise should have two 6kg foam fire extinguishers. Decanting petrol from one container to another is probably the task entailing the highest risk, so great care should be taken and obviously no one should be smoking (in any case, if it is a business, it would be against the law to smoke inside the enclosed space of an awning at any time). Even a spark from static electricity has been known to start a petrol fire, so be careful to be well earthed and not brush against nylon clothing beforehand.

Other potential hazards to consider include the following – though remember this is not an exhaustive list:

- Trips and falls – caused by obstacles, trailing cables, contamination
- Falling from a height – for example, putting up the awning
- Electrical safety – ensure you have correct wiring and earthing, approved generators
- Lifting and carrying – use the correct posture when lifting the kart
- Dropping tools or parts
- Control of chemicals and hazardous substances – ensure the instructions are kept safe in case of contamination of eyes or skin

PUBLIC LIABILITY INSURANCE

Having public liability insurance cover is strongly advised, and is a requirement if the enterprise is in any way a business venture. A private individual would be advised to check their household or vehicle insurance to see if their karting activities might be covered, but if in doubt, ask. The actual track activities will in the most case be covered by the indemnities signed by the driver – but as an example, what if an awning blows away in a gale and damages other vehicles or awnings?

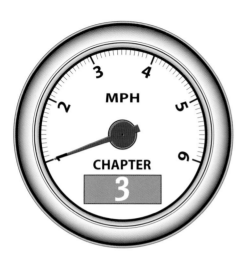

Looking After Your Kart

THE KART CHASSIS

Although a kart looks simple, with a steel frame and a wheel at each corner, it is actually quite complex with a range of possible adjustments. The controls consist of a brake pedal, a throttle pedal, a steering wheel, and if it is a gearbox (shifter) kart, then a clutch and gear-change lever. There might be an engine on/off switch, and if it is a TAG engine, then a starter button. 'TAG' stands for 'touch and go', which means it has an on-board electric starter motor, as opposed to the traditional older type of race kart where the kart is started by lifting the rear wheels off the ground and pushing until enough speed is gained to drop the kart and bump start the engine.

The MSA defines a kart as 'A small four-wheel racing vehicle with a rigid frame and no suspension of the wheels. The engine(s) drives the rear wheels only, and these rear wheels must be joined by a single-piece rear axle with no differential
action between them. The driver will be seated with feet to the fore.'

Kart Chassis Adjustments

The number of adjustments possible can be daunting, but the kart supplier or manufacturer should be able to give advice on a standard set-up. Once a good set-up has been found, deviations from this can be made for wet or dry weather, or track and weather conditions. Most

Plan view of a typical kart.

importantly keep a note of these settings, and the deviations tried with the effect of each. This will be a valuable resource each time that circuit is revisited. Pro-forma kart set-up sheets can be found on the web. Most of the possible adjustments in approximate order of importance as a deviation from the standard set-up are itemized below. Some of the terms may be unfamiliar, but will be explained later.

Adjustments of the following kart parts and settings are possible:

• Gearing – usually set so the engine reaches maximum rpm at the fastest part of the circuit
• Tyre pressures – wet or dry, and according to track temperature and weather
• Overall width of the rear wheels – the maximum is 140mm in most classes
• Overall width of the front wheels – change for wet or dry conditions
• Toe – toe-out more for wet conditions
• Camber/caster – this is adjusted on the front king pins

• Torsion bars – if available, whether fitted or not, orientation
• Seat – height and distance from the front, stiffness of the material
• Seat stays – the number and placement at each side
• Ballast – its placement
• Rear axle – its stiffness and length, its diameter, the number of bearings used
• Ackerman angle – alternative mounting points for the track rods
• Hubs – their length and material
• Wheel rims – their material: aluminium or magnesium alloy, width and offset
• Ride height – the front and rear may be adjustable
• Wheelbase – some karts can extend the wheelbase at the rear axle
• Brake balance – if simultaneous, four-wheel brakes as found in gearbox karts
• Internal gear ratios – if it is a geared class and permitted within the regulations
• Aerodynamic adjustments – generally only on the faster gearbox karts

Rear hub showing the locking screw.

Spacers are used on the front stub axle to adjust the width between the wheels.

Every adjustment must be tried on the track, as it may not result in the expected effect, even if proven from past experience. Try some extremes to see the effect they make: feel the difference or ask the driver's opinion. Remember that novice drivers will be less able to report accurately, so the team manager or mechanic must watch the kart on the track. In the end it is the stop-watch times that will determine if the change is beneficial or not.

Try pushing the kart along a smooth roadway in a straight line, with the chain removed if the engine does not have a clutch: it should roll along very freely. Now turn the steering wheel to one side and try pushing, and you will find it will be much harder. The reason for this is that the outer rear wheel must travel further than the inside wheel to turn the corner, and since the wheels are joined together by a single length of axle with no differential gear as found in cars, one of the wheels must skid. That will slow the kart down, so a kart is designed to lift the inside rear wheel off the ground in a corner, even if minimally, to reduce

friction. Much of the set-up on a kart is to optimize this inside rear-wheel lift, by how much and for how long.

When karts were simpler, narrowing the rear track (moving the rear wheels inwards) led to an increase in grip at the back, which tended to give more understeer. Conversely, moving the front wheels inwards to increase front end grip leads to more oversteer. However, modern karts with large diameter rear axles and very stiff chassis may well be different. Either way, moving the wheels in or out will have an effect. The rear hubs are adjusted by slackening a tension bolt and sliding the hub in or out on the axle. The front hubs are often set by adjusting the number of spacers between the inner part of the axle and the hub.

Understeer is when the kart tries to push on when the steering wheel is turned into a corner, and oversteer is when the rear of the kart loses grip and tries to swing round. In extreme circumstances, if it moves wide of the racing line front end first, that is understeer; if it is trying to spin and needs a lot of opposite-lock steering correction, that is oversteer.

FRONT END GEOMETRY

Steering on a kart is very direct. In most cases the steering wheel is bolted to a steering column, which is connected at the lower end to two track rods leading to the steering arms on the stub-axle hub assemblies. But the way these items are connected, and the angles of the arms and the stub-axle kingpin, are very important. Some larger gearbox karts may use a rack-and-pinion steering, like a car.

The steering on a kart is very direct.

Ackerman Angles

If the steering arms (part of the stub axle) were at right angles to the axle, and the track rods were mounted centrally on the steering column (one above the other), then there would be no Ackerman effect and one of the tyres would have to skid to go round a corner. Ackerman angle is introduced so that the inside front tyre has to describe a smaller radius circle on a corner than the outside front tyre, which has a longer arc to follow. It is done by angling the steering arms inwards and by fixing the inner ends of the track rods on a triangular mount on

the steering column. There may be an option of two or three holes on the steering arm for the outer ends of the track rods to effect further changes in angle.

When the line of the angles of each steering arm is extended backwards, if they intersect at the middle of the rear axle, the Ackerman angle is neutral or true. More Ackerman angle (the intersection forward of the rear axle) will lead to smoother but heavier steering; less Ackerman will lead to more direct, sharper steering. But the Ackerman angle is affected by the toe-in or toe-out of the kart as well.

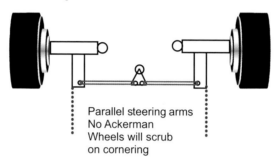

Parallel steering arms
No Ackerman
Wheels will scrub
on cornering

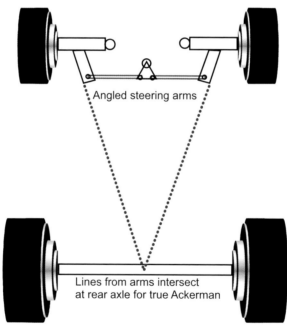

Angled steering arms

Lines from arms intersect
at rear axle for true Ackerman

More angled steering arms brings intersection
forward of the rear axle for more turn of inside wheel

Caster and Camber

The caster is the angle at which the kingpins (the bolts that secure the stub axle to the chassis) lie in relation to vertical. Camber is the attitude of the front wheels relative to vertical: if the tops of the front wheels are nearer the centre line of the kart than the bottom, that is negative camber, and if the tops are further out, that is positive camber. The starting position for most karts is to have neutral or no camber, or just a little, which might revert to no camber when the driver is seated in the kart on the ground.

When the front wheels are turned as if to take a corner, the combination of caster and Ackerman will have a jacking effect, to lift the inside rear wheel.

Larger caster angles will make for heavier steering and more jacking effect, and may be useful in the wet. Caster and camber may be fixed on simpler, more basic karts, but very often there are adjustable 'pills' on the top and bottom fixing of the kingpin: these allow variation of caster and camber, which inter-relate. These large washer-like 'pills' will have an offset central hole for the kingpin bolt, and a ring of smaller holes around the outside so it can be rotated for different caster and camber, then locked in place with a small screw.

When the steering is on full lock, the jacking effect lifts the inside rear wheel.

Adjuster 'pills' are used on the top and bottom of the front stub-axle supports to adjust camber and caster.

Measure between the tracking discs to check toe-out and camber.

Initial Set-up

With the kart on a stand, lock the steering wheel in the straight ahead position so that the centre-line of the arm on the steering column which connects to the track rods is directly above the centre-line of the kart. If possible replace the wheels with circular metal discs known as 'tracking discs': these will be more accurate than using the wheels.

Starting with all settings in their most neutral position and equal spacers in both stub axles, set the toe to neutral, so that the measurement between the front edge of the discs is exactly the same as the measurement between the rear-most edge of the discs. This means that the front wheels are parallel. A quick way to measure the toe is to scratch a cross in the middle of each tyre surface and measure the distance across with the crosses at the front, then rotate each tyre until the crosses are at the rear and measure again. Measure and note the distance between the top edge of the discs, and compare with the measurement between the bottom edge of the discs: this is the camber. It is negative if the top measurement is less than the bottom.

The rear axle should spin freely without a chain fitted, and the distance from the outer edge of the bearing hangar to the end of the axle should be exactly the same on both sides. Fit tracking discs or wheels with the hubs exactly the same distance out from the kart. Using a long, stiff straight-edge from the front discs, check that the gap to the rear tracking discs is identical on both sides: this will ensure the kart chassis is straight and true. The distance compared between the centre-line of the front to rear axle on both sides should be within 2 or 3mm.

Now with the engine fitted and the driver seated in the kart, check the front corner weights by putting the kart on a flat-bed surface, and putting identical scales under each front wheel: this will determine if there is any twist in the chassis. If there is, it is usually relatively easy to 'bounce' the kart straight by putting a block under the kingpin on the heavier front side and getting one or more heavy persons to stand on the back axle, whilst another bounces on the light front side until the front corner weights are identical.

Re-check all the measurements, then the kart will be set neutrally ready for adjustments at the track. There are proprietary laser alignment tools to make the task of measurement and adjustment much easier, but remember some measurements will change with the driver seated in the kart on the ground.

Replacing a Rear Axle

After the old axle has been removed, depending on the design, either fit the bearings over the new axle in roughly the correct positions, or slide the axle into the bearings already fitted to the kart with the fixing screws not quite pinched up. Remember to fit first any water-pump belts, brake disc and holder and any sprocket carrier which are between the bearings before fitting these. Also slip on spare water-pump belts if a water

pump is used; these can be taped on to the axle to be used in case of a breakage. Similarly with certain four-stroke engines using an inboard sprocket, a spare chain may be slipped over the axle and fixed out of the way.

Once the bearing hangers are in place, pinch up the outermost pair, adjust the axle so it is equidistant on each side, and tighten the bearing fixing bolts ensuring the axle can spin freely at all times. Make sure the distance from the front kingpin is the same on both sides, then tighten any third bearing hangar fixing bolts, again ensuring the axle remains free. Apply thread-locking compound to the grub screws in the bearings and tighten them down. Some mechanics like to centre punch and just indent the axle with a drill before fixing the grub screws. It can be a good idea to wrap some tape over the top of the grub screws as another aid to preventing them falling out.

Laser gauges can replace the traditional tape measure.

SEAT FITTING

First of all, however, the driver must be made comfortable in the kart, whilst the seat must be put in the best position to optimize the handling. It's actually more important to have the seat in the best position for good handling, even if driver comfort is compromised a little. Therefore optimize the seat position first and move the pedals and steering wheel to suit. Most chassis manufacturers will offer standard measurements for fitting a seat, usually from the front tube where the heel would rest, to the front edge of the seat, and from the rear axle surface to the top lip of the seat.

This set-up is fine for a middle-sized seat made for professional drivers, but seats do not just get wider, so big and small drivers, or users of a different shaped seat, will end up out of position. A better way is to take a point to one side of the spine relief channel that runs down the back of the seat (the spine channels vary in depth) to the nearest point on the axle. For instance, Tillett Racing Seats recommend this measurement to be 185mm on pre-2005 karts, 175mm on pre-2009 karts, and 160mm on today's karts. But note that children or very short drivers may not be able to quite achieve this measurement.

Seats come in many shapes and forms, offering different stiffness, with or without flat bottoms, with or without full or partial padding, and of course in different sizes. It is important to be very snugly fitted, so try before buying, and wear the normal racesuit and rib protector if worn, when trying for fit. Basically it should not be possible to fit your fingers between your body and any part of the seat: it should be tight to the point of being uncomfortable, otherwise there is the risk of damage to the ribs. A 10mm block should be put under the seat, to give ground clearance.

If the seat is being fitted on the stand, then fit the seat 5mm below the chassis tubes: this is a safe dimension. Make sure the four metal stay tabs are parallel to the composite of the seat surface; if they are not, bend them with a big adjustable spanner. Then fit the seat to the correct dimensions; most seats will have a small flat area to give the angle the seat was designed to run at. Use a 40mm hard nylon or steel washer at each fixing point, as it is important to prevent stay penetration in an incident – in any case this is a mandatory requirement. If there is a gap, fill it with correctly fitting spacers. Never use soft rubber – always use solid hard plastic or aluminium spacers.

The seat-fitting measurement from the rear axle to the back of the seat.

There are two important measurements when fitting a seat, from front to seat lip as shown here.

Steering Wheel Adjustment

Steering on a kart should be done using the large shoulder muscles for power, not primarily the arm muscles, so the seat should not be too laid back. The steering-column height can usually be adjusted downwards by putting the top support mount upside down. The length of the column can be shortened by sawing a few centimetres off the top and re-drilling the steering-wheel boss fixing point, or in some cases there are two mounting points on the boss. Also extralong columns can be purchased. An angled steering-wheel boss can be purchased, so the top part of the steering wheel is brought closer to the driver. Always mount the steering wheel with the third spoke upwards, to reduce injury to the ribcage if it makes contact with the driver in an accident.

The driver's elbows should be bent in his normal position for holding the steering wheel.

Pedal Adjustment

There is a limited range of adjustment possible to the pedals by adjusting the stop bolts and at the same time shortening or lengthening the throttle cable, or brake rod or cable; that is usually enough adjustment for the average driver. For drivers with shorter legs, various types of pedal extender can be used, from the type that slips over the pedal, through to the type that moves the whole assembly backwards. It should be possible for the driver to press the pedals fully, especially the brake, without fully straightening the leg.

Drivers with short legs could use a slip-on pedal adjuster.

THE INTERNAL COMBUSTION ENGINE

Most karts use an internal combustion engine, either two-stroke or four-stroke or even a rotary engine, although some may use an electric motor powered by a recharge-able battery. Two-stroke engines are simpler and have a better power-to-weight ratio than four-stroke engines, but four-stroke engines may be designed to have a much longer life between rebuilds. Corporate 'arrive-and-drive' karts for general public use are generally powered by four-stroke engines because they need less maintenance, do not need to be high powered, and run on pure petrol or

gas. Two-stroke engines, on the other hand, may run to much higher revolutions per minute (rpm) and need an oil mixed in with the fuel for lubrication.

Reciprocating internal combustion engines have one or more cylinders within which a piston moves up and down, its motion converted to circular by the attachment of the connecting rod to the crankshaft. When the piston is at the top of its stroke, having compressed a fuel and air mix drawn in through a carburettor, or by a fuel injection system, the spark plug fires and pushes the piston downwards as the mixture burns. The next time the piston comes up it pushes the burnt gases out of the exhaust pipe.

An air-cooled two-stroke engine cutaway. (Courtesy Tal-Ko)

Two-stroke Engines

The two-stroke or two-cycle engine is the favourite for racing karts on account of its good power-to-weight ratio and simplicity. As the piston is pushed down by the fuel burning, the exhaust gases leave by the exhaust ports, basically strategically placed holes in the cylinder wall, and simultaneously the new charge of fuel and air mix is drawn in through the inlet ports ready for the next explosion as the piston returns upwards.

So the spark plug fires every time the piston goes up, usually just before it gets to the top, to give time to ignite the mixture just before the maximum compression. There is always some leakage of the new mixture charge across to the exhaust pipe, but the exhaust pipes are specially shaped to cause a reflection back to the cylinder, which helps to keep the new mixture inside the cylinder.

There are various methods of bringing the fuel and air mixture into the engine: the simplest is piston port induction, where the piston alone uncovers and covers the ports used to bring the mixture in from the carbu-

rettor. However, the reed valve intake is now the most common. The crankcase under the piston in a two-stroke engine is sealed, so as the piston moves up it draws a new fuel/air charge into the crankcase space, then when it moves down that charge is transferred to the top of the piston via transfer ports. The reeds close and prevent the charge escaping back towards the carburettor.

The final method used in karts is a rotary valve intake, where a circular disc with shaped cut-outs driven by the crankshaft is used to allow the mixture to enter, then closed to prevent leakage.

Because the crankcase is sealed there is no oil sump, so the lubrication of the moving parts is usually carried out by mixing the petrol with a certain amount of oil. Some of the oil will be burnt and the exhaust may be slightly smoky, or blue in colour. Modern synthetic oils, as used in the more modern types of water-cooled engine, greatly reduce this effect. Two-stroke kart engines can rotate up to 20,000 times per second, but most modern engines are rev-limited to achieve better reliability.

A modern, water-cooled two-stroke engine with the piston at the bottom of its stroke.

The engine cut-away, with the piston at the top of its stroke, and the spark plug about to fire.

Four-stroke Engines

The four-stroke engine has many more moving parts, and unless very highly tuned, will generally be a larger size, and thus heavier, than a two-stroke engine for the same power output. Mechanically actuated valves are used to control the intake and exhaust. When the piston moves down as the mixture burns, all the valves are closed. The next time the piston rises, the exhaust valve opens and lets the exhaust gases escape down the exhaust pipe. When the piston moves down again, the inlet valve opens and allows the new fuel/air charge to enter the cylinder. The next time the piston rises, the valves are both closed, compressing the mixture ready for the spark plug to fire.

Thus the spark plug only fires every second time the piston rises, or on every fourth stroke. Most large kart engines are rev-limited, because if the speed of the engine is too great, catastrophic failure can take place within the valve gear, leading to a lot of expensive damage. Properly maintained, a four-stroke engine offers long life between rebuilds.

Clutch and Starters

Most modern non-gearbox kart engines incorporate a centrifugal clutch. This allows the engine to tick over to allow the kart to remain stationary until the accelerator or throttle is pressed down, increasing the speed of the engine, engaging the clutch and delivering drive through a chain or belt to the rear wheels. Prior to the general adoption of centrifugal clutches, the drive to the rear wheels was directly from the crankshaft, so karts had to be started by helpers lifting the rear wheels, running with the kart until sufficient speed was obtained, then dropping the kart on to the ground whilst still pushing to start the engine. The kart engine is stopped by braking to a standstill – it cannot run whilst the kart is stationary.

When the engine has a clutch, the engine can be started by either a retractable pull cord, an on-board electric motor starter, or a plug-in external electric starter which is removed once the engine is running.

Gearbox Engines

If the engine has a gearbox then the rotation of the crankshaft is transferred through a clutch by primary gears, then into the gearbox. In this case the clutch is manually operated by a hand or foot control. The clutch allows the motion of the engine to be temporarily disconnected from the gearbox so the gears can be engaged. The gears are changed sequentially, so there is a neutral between first and second gear, allowing the clutch to be released with no drive to the rear wheels so it can tick over at standstill.

The sequential gearstick lever is moved in one direction to engage first gear, then in the other direction

The gearstick is a lever to the side of the steering wheel.

to engage in turn second, third and so on. When slowing down and coming back down through the gears, the gearstick is moved in the opposite direction. It springs back into a middle position after each movement. The KZ class 125cc gearbox engines have a six-speed gearbox, as do the very powerful twin-cylinder 250cc engines. Motocross bike engines used for the 250 National class may have five or six gears; the exception to the rule is the Rotax DD2 engine, which has only two gears and a centrifugal clutch.

In most cases on gearbox karts the clutch is only used to move off from a standstill, and is not required to change gear.

BASIC MAINTENANCE

It is very important to keep the kart clean if only to spot any cracks or potential failures that may develop. Some components should be changed on a routine basis, after a certain number of races or practice days. Fuel should be drained out of the tank and stored in a sealed container at the end of the day or weekend, preferably minimizing the amount of air within the container by keeping it reasonably full; that way it will be reuseable for a reasonable length of time, although some competitors will always use freshly mixed two-stroke fuel for each new race weekend. Always dispose of used fuel safely and legally, by finding a garage or recycle centre that is able to take it.

Cleaning the Kart

To clean the kart, give it a good spray all over with a proprietary multi-purpose maintenance spray, which will have water-dispersant properties – though be careful not to spray the brake pads. In the long run it will be more cost effective to purchase a 5ltr can, and decant it into a suitable spraying canister, than continually buying aerosol cans. At the same time buy a 5ltr can of brake cleaner fluid; if it has been a wet race, spray the kart as soon as possible and before putting it away. Normally it is better to remove the engine and other major components before cleaning the kart between race weekends.

Every so often strip the kart down, removing the whole rear axle assembly as well, the better to clean the awkward nooks and crannies. Some teams will do this every night at the track. Brush the cleaning fluid into all the corners and wipe the kart clean. Only use a power washer if the components with bearings are removed first. As you wipe the kart, check for cracks, loose nuts and bolts, broken springs, frayed cables and so on. Then use brake cleaner on the brake discs to remove any traces of the maintenance spray, and clean the discs with emery cloth.

Some competitors will cut back the rubber seals on axle bearings and wash out the lubricating grease, replacing it with a light machine oil. They do this to reduce friction – though be aware that the bearings will then require more frequent maintenance and replacement.

The Chain

The drive chain should be sprayed with chain grease just after the kart comes back from a track session, as the chain will be warm and the grease will penetrate better. If a chain with O-rings is used, ensure the correct type of chain oil is applied: this type of chain will need less maintenance but it does absorb more horsepower so is best suited to endurance racing. At the end of the day remove the chain and carefully clean it with a soft brush and some lubricant. Check each link for binding, and in time the wear can be assessed by seeing how much the chain can be twisted sideways. If in doubt, replace the chain.

Then check the sprockets: when the teeth start to become hooked they are overdue for replacement. Check the sprocket on the axle for run-out – this means it weaves from side to side. If excessive the fault could be in either the sprocket itself or the sprocket carrier, so replace as necessary. To align the sprockets, take a steel ruler or similar straight-edge and with the engine mounted and tight, slide the sprocket carrier on the axle until the two sprockets are aligned with the straight-edge just touching the teeth on the front sprocket. Average out any slight run-out.

To move the sprocket carrier it may be necessary to loosen the bolts holding the sprocket to it, as well as the pinch bolt on the carrier – but tighten them each time during the alignment process. Then fit the chain and adjust the tension by loosening and sliding the engine on

Lining up the drive sprockets with a straight-edge.

the chassis tubes until the chain has about 10mm of up-and-down movement on its longest length, with the engine tightened down, of course. If the chain is too long to allow correct tension, one or more links may need to be removed, although chains can be purchased in varying lengths. A chain-splitter tool will be required which pushes the pins out of a link, and allows one or more links to be removed.

When reassembling, use a ball-pein hammer to reclose the rivets. Rotate the axle completely whilst checking for any tight spots on the chain; if there are, either the chain, the sprocket or the carrier may need replacing, or the axle itself may be slightly bent. Finally, respray the chain with lubricant.

Cables

A cable will almost certainly operate the throttle. A cable may operate the brake, and if the kart is of the gearbox variety, a cable will most likely operate the clutch. Brake and clutch cables will be of larger diameter and stronger than the throttle cable. Cable inners must also be used as a safety strap on the brake rod, and may be used as

safety straps on the exhaust or rear bumper in case the attachment springs or bolts come off. Some drivers remove the nylon inner tube to reduce friction. The cable may have to be cut to an appropriate length, both inner and outer. One end of a cable will have a nipple which slots into the throttle body or lever, or the clutch lever as appropriate. Solderless nipples can be purchased as well. At the pedal end, the cable inner is threaded through an eyelet on the pedal, looped back on itself and secured with two cable clamps. The best sort is the flat variety, but brass electrical connectors are often used, removed from 'chocolate blocks'. A short length of fuel pipe can be used to protect the inner from wear where it is looped through the pedal eyelet. Inners and outer can usually be purchased separately, so the inner can be changed more often as it becomes frayed with constant adjustment of the clamps.

Throttle Cable

The throttle cable connects the throttle body or the throttle-operating lever to the pedal, and the inner is

A throttle pedal has two stops, one for the relaxed position and one for the full open position.

threaded through an adjuster at the lug on the chassis where the outer is terminated, then to the pedal where it is looped back and clamped on itself, with any excessive cable cut off. In the off position, the pedal stop is adjusted so the driver's leg is bent sufficiently to operate the full movement and still allow the leg not to be over-stretched. In the full throttle position, the other pedal stop is adjusted so the cable is taut but not over-stretched so as to bend the lever on the carburettor but still allow for the full opening of the throttle butterfly or slide.

Check this frequently during a race weekend. The adjuster on the chassis lug can be used for fine adjustments. There should be a return spring on the pedal, and on the throttle lever.

Brake Cable or Rod

A cable or a rod may operate the brake master cylinder. Either way it is mandatory to use a safety cable loop, or to have two cables in parallel in case one breaks. The safety loop must be a cable of at least 1.8mm diameter and tension just after the pedal is fully extended.

The pedal stop is adjusted so the pedal sits comfortably upright with the driver's knee bent sufficiently that the brake pedal can be depressed fully and not quite fully extend the driver's leg. A return spring is used to pull the pedal back. There is no stop on the extended position, and the pedal must not reach over the top of the front bumper bar.

The brake pedal must have a secondary safety strap.

Clutch Cable

The clutch may be either hand operated, mounted on the steering wheel hub, or a pedal layout like a car. The cable is adjusted so the clutch can open sufficiently not to cause drag on the engine.

BRAKE MAINTENANCE

Brakes are critical safety components on a kart, and must be maintained carefully and expertly. The brake pads are squeezed against a rotating disc, which is fixed securely to the front wheel hub or rear axle as appropriate. The pads are operated by pairs of pistons in the brake callipers, usually operated by hydraulic pressure, or sometimes on lower powered karts by levers connected to cables that run to the foot pedal. When hydraulically operated, a cable or rod links the brake pedal to a lever on the master cylinder. That lever pushes a piston to generate high pressure on the brake fluid piped to the brake callipers. Any air or moisture in the brake fluid will compromise the operation, so it is important to be scrupulously clean when working on brake parts.

First ensure that the brake disc or rotor is centrally located between the two halves of the calliper. On the rear axle this is achieved by loosening the clamping screw on the brake disc carrier and sliding it along the axle until it is in the correct position. It may be necessary to loosen slightly the screws fixing the disc to the carrier, to release the tension. Sometimes the discs are said to be floating, which means the mounting fasteners allow some sideways movement to help with self alignment. Carefully examine the discs for cracks, undue wear, or damage from contact with the ground. Re-tighten the fixing and clamping screws, then check there is no excessive run-out – a sideways movement when the disc is rotated. Operate the brake pedal and the pads should move evenly on to the disc. If the pedal feels spongy then the system may need to be bled to remove any air bubbles.

It is very important to use the correct type of brake fluid, either Dot 5 silicon or Dot 4 or 5.1 glycol based, and never mix the two types. If the wrong type of brake fluid is used it can attack the integrity of the seals and lead to eventual leakage and failure. Always keep the spare brake fluid in its sealed container, and do not shake it before use. The master cylinder may have a top-up

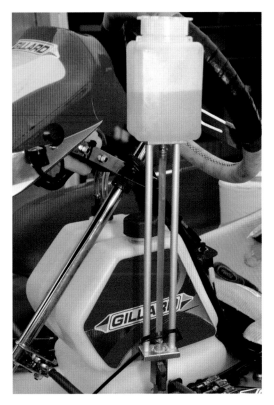

Bleeding the brakes, using a tall external reservoir.

The brake-bleeding nipple on a calliper.

reservoir like a car, in which case it is easy to add fluid directly. More usually the system is sealed; the brake rod or cable is disconnected, so the piston in the master cylinder is fully relaxed. Then the filling screw is carefully removed, and a reservoir on a long extension fitted in its place. That is used to give enough height to push fluid through the system when the tap on the pipe is opened.

Fill the reservoir and open the bleed screws on each calliper in turn, starting with the one furthest away. Fix a tube over the bleed screw to drain the excess fluid into a bottle; always dispose of it safely and legally. Allow fluid to flow through the bleed screw until it is clean and free of tiny bubbles, then tighten the bleed screw and move on to the next one. When finished, close the tap on the temporary reservoir and refit the filling screws on the master cylinder. Re-connect the brake pedal and check the operation of the pads.

The brake rod may be adjustable in length to suit the reach of the driver's leg, and once adjusted, there must be a safety cable alongside in case the rod breaks. The pads may need to be adjusted so they sit just clear of the brake disc when relaxed. Too big a gap and the pedal will have to be pressed too far, perhaps running out of travel on the pedal or brake master cylinder. Too little clearance, and the pads may make contact with the disc as the axle flexes in corners.

Various different systems are used to adjust the pads. Shims may have to be inserted behind each pad, or may be taken out between the two halves of the calliper. The pads will have to be replaced when worn. Various methods of fixing the pad are used, sometimes screws locating into the metal backing piece, sometimes pins through holes in the pads. It is very important to replace any locking pins, split pins or locking wire. If the seals in the pistons need replacing this can be done, but again the utmost cleanliness is required before reassembly.

If the brake disc protrudes below the chassis tubes, it will likely be mandatory to fit a brake protector. This is a hard rubber of plastic skid plate, designed so that the brake disc is protected from scraping on kerbs.

A disc protector must be fitted if the disc protrudes below the chassis.

SAFETY

Before going out on to the track, always double check that the wheel nuts are tight, the engine clamps are tight, the wheel hubs are tight on the axles, the brakes work, the seat is fixed securely, any ballast is secure, there are no cracks in any parts such as axles, the tyres are inflated to the correct pressures, and there are no fluid leaks. If the front wheel rims are the type with bearings in the actual wheel, then the large nyloc nut on the end of the stub axle should be tightened up, then slackened just enough so the wheel can spin freely. There must always be at least one or two threads showing on the end of the stub axle, outside the lock nut.

Pay attention to all other fasteners, such as those fixing the floor tray to the chassis. Secure the clips that hold the front fairing to the front bumper with cable ties. In critical races it is advisable to use throttle or clutch cable secured with clamps, and threaded loosely over components that are held on with springs, such as exhaust pipes; then if the spring breaks, the cable may be enough to hold the component together until the end of the race.

REPLACING CRITICAL COMPONENTS

There are various fasteners – screws and nuts – which must be replaced by new ones on a regular basis, some because they are continually loosened and tightened for adjustment, some because they are in a load-bearing safety critical area. Failure to do this will result in eventual breakage, which at worst could lead to a crash, at best a non-finish. The same replacement ethos applies to springs and cables. Locking nuts, like nylocs, should only be refitted twice, once as new and maybe one more time, and it should always be possible to see a thread or two of the screw or bolt through the locking nut. Keep a note of when these safety critical components are replaced.

At least once a year go over the entire kart replacing nuts and bolts. Buy these in bulk from a fasteners wholesaler.

Other items which need to be replaced on a regular basis are bearings, chains, sprockets, fuel pipes, the fuel filter and water hosepipes and clips. Don't forget the fuel pipe inside the fuel tank, which terminates on a brass weight used to counter surge in the corners. And for clutched engines, the clutch plates or shoes will wear out.

FACT

Safety critical fasteners

- Wheel rim attachment lock nuts, and stub-axle lock nut
- Steering-wheel hub to steering-column fixing bolt
- Clamping screws in axle hubs
- Clamping screws in brake disc carrier
- Sidepod to chassis fixing bolts or springs
- Front steering-hub kingpin bolts
- Brake disc attachment bolts and nuts

FITTING AND REPLACING TYRES

An inevitable task for the driver or mechanic is to change a set of tyres on the wheel rims. Firstly the air is let out of the tyre by removing the valve core (with a special tool), and any bead retainers removed (these are small screws fitted through the shoulders of the wheel rim to project behind the bead of the tyre, to prevent it slipping off under the high G forces found during cornering). A special tyre bead breaker is used to push the tyre bead off each side of the rim.

With the opposite sides of the tyre pushed into the middle well of the rim, the rear side of the tyre is levered over the edge of the rim, then pulled off. The remaining sidewall follows.

Clean the inside of the rim, removing any rubber deposits, and apply some tyre soap to the new tyre and the inside shoulders of the rim. It's helpful if the tyre is slightly warm, at least not cold, to make it more pliable to fit. Some tyres have the rotation direction marked on them, so before fitting make sure the two fronts are fitted in opposite directions, and likewise for the two rears.

Lay the tyre on a clean piece of surface and work the inner edge of the rim into the tyre – in other words, the outer edge of the rim will be upwards. Then reverse the wheel, and keeping the sidewall that is already fitted in the well of the rim, kneel on the inner side of the tyre, and with fingers and thumbs work the other sidewall into the rim. You

Tools for Kart Maintenance

Karts can be maintained with a minimum of basic tools as shown below: the more essential items are at the top, and items which might be borrowed when necessary further down. One of the readily available multi-socket/ratchet/spanner sets and a screwdriver set would probably cover most needs, along with some specialist items.

- Tyre pressure gauge
- Spark plug spanner
- Foot pump
- Fire extinguisher
- Stop watch
- 10mm ring/open-ended spanner
- 13mm ring/open-ended spanner
- 17mm ring/open-ended spanner
- 19mm ring/open-ended spanner
- 10mm T-bar socket
- 13mm T-bar socket
- Rubber hammer
- Selection of screwdrivers
- Allen key set (metric)
- Filtered fuel filler funnel
- Fuel can
- Mixing jug calibrated in ml
- Steel rulers (two)
- Tape measure 3m
- Combination pliers
- Long nose pliers
- Side cutters
- Battery drill
- Set of drill pieces
- Hacksaw
- Craft knife

- Circlip pliers (internal/external)
- Large socket for front wheel hubs
- Chain splitter
- Air compressor
- Ball pein hammer
- Tyre bead breaker
- Tyre valve core removal tool
- Tyre levers (small)
- Torque wrench
- Laser alignment tool
- Tap and die set (metric)

In addition a number of fluids will be required:

- Fuel
- Chain lube spray
- Two-stroke racing oil
- General maintenance spray
- Degreaser
- Brake cleaner
- Brake fluid
- Carb cleaner
- Loctite
- Cleaner for plastics
- Water repellent for visor
- Polish
- Gasket sealant
- Gear oil
- Multi-purpose or 'moly' grease
- Anti-seize copper grease/lubricant
- Water for radiator (if liquid-cooled engine)
- Antifreeze for winter conditions (if permitted)
- Silicon sealer (for exhaust)

A suggested toolkit for karting.

A tyre-changing contest.

A bead breaker is used to push the tyre sidewalls off the rim.

Taking a tyre off the rim.

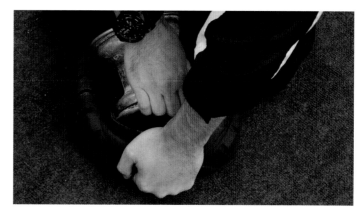

may need to raise the side of the wheel furthest from you, and you may need to push the middle of the tread into a V shape to keep the sidewalls in the well of the wheel rim.

Refit any bead retainers, but only screw them flush with the inner side of the rim at this stage. Check if the sealing washers are in good condition: if not, replace them. Also replace the tyre valve if in doubt. Inflate the tyre until each side pops on to the rim, taking care not to exceed the maximum pressure marked on the tyre, then finish screwing in the bead retainers. The rims will pop on more easily if the tyre core is left out at this stage. When inflating the tyres, if you have access to a correct-sized metal casing, put them inside this so as to keep the running surface flat. Then refit the tyre core and set the tyre to the correct pressure.

The best mechanics do not use tyre levers, they only use their fingers and thumbs. Alternatively special tools can be purchased to remove the tyres from the rims. Competitions are sometimes held for tyre changing, with the best participants taking four tyres off the rims and replacing them in about thirty seconds.

Balancing Tyres

When a new tyre is fitted the wheels should be balanced, especially at high speed tracks. So long as the wheel bearings are very free, the fronts can be balanced on the kart. Start the wheel rotating slowly and wait until it comes to a stop. Fit a balance weight to the top side of the inner surface of the wheel and try again, repeating until the wheel stops at random places. The balance weight can be fixed on with sticky tape at this stage, until the right

size is determined. If too much weight is attached, the wheel will rotate on its own until the weight is at the bottom side. The stick-on balance weights can be purchased in strips of various sizes. The rears will have to be balanced using a special tyre-balancing jig to which the wheel can be fixed, allowing for free rotation. Check the balance on each tyre after the first session of use.

INSURANCE

There are plenty of companies that specialize in insurance for race and kart equipment. It is probably going to be necessary to leave the kart at a race track overnight, and the basic insurance would cover theft, but make sure that any conditions such as alarms on garages, tents, vans or trailers are strictly adhered to. Insurance can even be extended to cover damage during racing, at extra cost, or maybe just if the kart is a complete write-off – though inevitably there will be an excess to pay, so see if it makes sense.

Check if some public liability cover is included: for instance, who would pay if an awning blew away in a strong wind and damaged other property or persons? Some insurance policies will cover loss of race wear, a licence replacement if lost or stolen, or refund entry fees if unable to race because of loss. Always keep records of all serial numbers of engines, karts, stopwatches and trailers.

In addition to public liability and property insurance, those in employment should ensure they are covered for loss of earnings, and that their life insurance covers the sport. This is even more important for racing abroad, where the travel insurance needs to be specially extended.

Driving Techniques and Testing

THE RACING LINE

Driving on a race track is unlike driving on a road: for a start, no one is supposed to be coming from the other direction, so the full width of the track must be used. This leads us on to describing the 'racing line': the line the kart should follow which gives the fastest time. It may vary in different weather and track conditions, perhaps substantially so in the wet. Deviations from the optimum racing line are sometimes required, for instance to execute an overtake.

Corners can be split into three basic phases: braking in a straight line up to the turn-in point; turning in and aiming for the apex of the corner; and finally the acceleration and exit phase.

The Braking Phase

To brake in a straight line up to the turn-in point, the kart should be positioned as far over to the opposite side of the track as possible from the direction of the corner. If the previous corner exit has been in the other direction, then gradually ease the kart over to the other side as gently as possible, using as little steering input as possible. Look for possible markers at the side of the track so that later braking points can be tried out on subsequent laps, mentally resetting the marker if necessary.

Apply the brake firmly and powerfully up to the point where the wheels are not quite locking up, at the same time releasing the throttle pedal. The maximum braking effect is when the wheels are almost locking up and

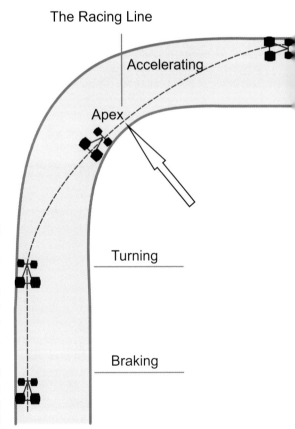

The Racing Line

Accelerating

Apex

Turning

Braking

Hairpin racing line.

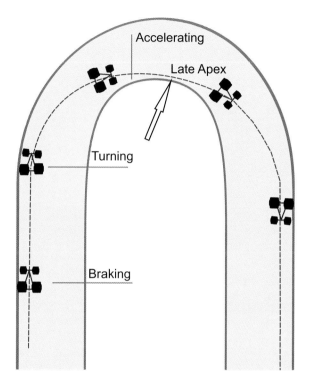

skidding. If they do lock, release the brake effort slightly until they unlock and start rotating again. Release the brake just at the point of starting to turn the steering wheel towards the corner.

Turning In

Once the brake is completely released, the kart should be aimed for the apex of the corner: on a simple corner this will be the midpoint of the arc of the corner, or perhaps slightly later. Gentle throttle application can be applied.

The Exit Phase

Once at the apex the throttle should be opened to the fullest extent compatible with the kart not breaking grip. The kart should be allowed to drift over to the opposite side of the track, running up and slightly over any kerbing if practical. The earliest the power can be applied from the apex of the corner the better for straight-line speed, and possible over-

taking. The kart has now been driven along the racing line for the corner, and as each corner is considered in the same way, and the racing line joined up all around the track, the fastest possible line will emerge. Watch the lines the experts take, and adjust accordingly the line you take.

Hairpin Bends

Driving hairpin bends can be tricky. Firstly the apex speed is likely to be lower, so more braking is required. In general the braking phase should slightly overshoot the classical line, and the apex point should be slightly later, all with the object of applying the power earlier for the exit phase. But doing so exposes the kart to another driver barrelling up the inside in a block overtake, so the line to be taken depends partly on whether the driver is trying for the best lap time to catch another kart, or defending against another kart. A block overtake is when the overtaking kart leaves the other with no immediate possible route back on to the racing line for the exit.

More Complex Corners

In a sequence of corners, the true racing line in one corner may have to be compromised in order to achieve a better line at the end of the sequence. Generally the aim is to achieve the fastest exit speed on to the straight.

OVERSTEER AND UNDERSTEER

If the kart crashes backwards into the barriers, or goes into a spin, then it has been oversteering, whereas if it crashes front first, then that is probably caused by understeer. If when the steering wheel is turned into a corner, the rear of the kart is threatening to whip round, that is oversteer. If the steering has to have more and more lock applied to make the kart turn into the corner, then that is understeer.

How to adjust the kart in order to counter these problems will be discussed in more detail later in the chapter.

Oversteering means the back of the kart slides more than the front, requiring opposite-lock steering.

Understeering means the front lacks grip, and the steering has to be turned more than is desirable.

WET WEATHER RACING

If one thing is certain in kart racing, it is that sooner or later there will be a wet practice or race. Wet weather grooved tyres will then be mounted, and in general terms the front wheels will be set as far out as possible, and the rear wheels will be set slightly closer together than they would be when used for the slicks. This is often achieved by using wheel rims that have a different offset to the rims used for the slicks. This means that the centre portion of the wheel's rim, where it is bolted on to the hub, is manufactured so that for the front rims it is nearer the inside edge of the rim to push the wheels outwards, and for the rear wheels it is more likely to be in the middle of the rim. The tyre pressures are also adjusted and set higher than they would be when used for the slicks.

Wet Set-up

If there is time to make adjustments to the kart, then generally more toe-out is applied. This gives the tyres a bit more 'scrubbing' effect on the straights, and helps to keep some heat in the tyre on the straights, ready for the next corner. Full castor is applied, if adjustable, and this helps with the jacking effect to lift the inside rear wheel. The front ride height may be raised as well. The gearing may be changed as the kart will be slower.

If allowed, shields may be fitted in front of the air box so water doesn't enter the carburettor so easily. Similarly a shield may be fitted in front of the rear disc, to help keep it dry. A proprietary water-repellent spray can be used on the wiring and ignition parts; however, do not spray inside the spark-plug cap as it could slip off too easily in the race. Part of the radiator may be blocked off

A wetsuit is worn in wet weather.

as less cooling will be needed. If the kart has four-wheel simultaneous braking as in the gearbox classes, the brake balance must be shifted towards the rear.

If the kart is carrying ballast, this could be mounted higher on the seat to move the centre of gravity up, and help to put extra weight on the outside rear tyre. Similarly if there is time, the seat itself might be raised so the driver's weight is used to the same effect.

In the past karts used to be softened off, but modern wet tyres can achieve so much grip that the kart is generally kept on quite stiff settings even in the wet.

Driver Aids

For the driver, a wetsuit is a must, to keep the racesuit as dry as possible. Wetsuits are one-piece nylon or can be clear plastic material so that the logos on the racesuit can still be seen.

Optional are slip-on rubber overshoes, and waterproof rubber or vinyl gloves. Some drivers fix on a whirly visor over the top of their normal visor; with these, the air pressure from the kart's movement spins the visor so the rain is thrown off to the side. Otherwise a good anti-fog solution can be applied to the inside of the normal visor, and an anti-rain solution on the outside so the rain just streams off. If spectacles are worn, put them and the crash helmet on for a few minutes before the race in order to give time for the temperature to equalize, because it is likely that they will steam up when first fitted.

Driving on a Wet Track

In wet conditions braking distances will be lengthened, corner speeds and maximum speeds will be less, and lap times will increase. During dry racing the slick tyres will deposit a rubbery line on the normal racing line, but once wet this area can become very slippery – which is why the fastest wet weather racing line might be quite different from the dry weather line. Karts may run wider round the outside of the corner in order to avoid the rubber deposits and gain more traction. Alternatively the best line might be to hook the inside wheels over a kerb and keep a very tight line.

Often the racing line will be round the outside of the corner, avoiding the slippery rubbery line made by the slicks.

If the wheels lock up on braking, then the brake must be quickly released to allow the wheels to rotate once more, then gently but firmly reapplied to reduce speed. It is much easier to spin out in the wet.

Approaching a corner it might be necessary to turn the steering into the corner earlier, and wait for the front end to grip once the tyre heats up and achieves grip.

If the track and the racing line start to dry out, wet weather tyres are more likely to overheat, and in the extreme could wear very rapidly, leaving little or no tread at the end of the race. In this situation drivers will search for puddles to cool the tyres. If the track looks as if it may dry out during the race, and it is still too wet to mount slicks, part-worn wets are best with the tyre pressures set a lot lower than normal.

AERODYNAMICS

Aerodynamic aids are generally only used on the faster gearbox karts. A rear wing is used to apply aerodynamic pressure – downforce – to the rear wheels to increase grip in the corners at the expense of some drag on the straights. A large front fairing is used to balance the kart and apply downforce to the front tyres.

FACT

Coaching

Every driver can benefit from coaching, especially novices. A good driver coach is well worth the extra expense, and new drivers would be well advised to book a course at a reputable kart school, or with a good coach. Lessons learned at the beginning of one's driving career will help to avoid common beginner's mistakes. Several of the members of the MSA recognized Association of Racing Kart Schools (ARKS) have their own race teams, and all their instructors have raced themselves to a high level.

The angle of the wing or front fairing determines how much downforce is applied at speed: the more the angle, the greater the downforce at the expense of drag on the straights. Often there is a small vertical tab or flap mounted upwards on the rear of the wing, called a Gurney flap. When deployed it can increase low to medium speed downforce but often at the expense of drag, and is no more than 2 per cent of the chord of the

A long-circuit superkart, showing the aerodynamic front nose fairing and rear wing.

wing. So a compromise must be reached between downforce for faster speeds round the corners, and reduction in drag which will increase top speeds. At short-circuit speeds the effect of downforce is still relevant, but not to so much extent. Perhaps more important is to reduce drag – for instance, getting the driver to tuck down behind the steering wheel on the straights.

TESTING

The most important aid to your test sessions is your notebook and pen, to record every setting and every change. Pro-forma set-up sheets are also easily sourced on the world-wide web. Try not to make more than one change per session otherwise the effect might be masked; however, you could quickly run out of time so sometimes the rule must be broken. Remember to note down the weather conditions as well. The air temperature will affect track temperature, which in turn will influence

your choice of tyre pressures. The barometric pressure and perhaps humidity will have a large influence on the jetting, and the wind direction and strength will have an influence on the top speed achievable on the straights, and hence the optimum gearing.

Prepping the Kart

Before going out to the track there are some essential tasks and checks to make: for instance, are the brakes working properly, is the seat secure, are the steering track rods free to operate and not locking up when the steering is at full lock? Are the wheel nuts tight, are the tyre pressures set? Do the kart and driver together weigh approximately the class weight? It is very unsafe to send a small driver out with the kart seriously underweight, as it will be too fast on the straights compared with the other karts, and the driver may not have the experience to handle it safely round the corners. Mount appropriate blocks of ballast until it weighs in correctly.

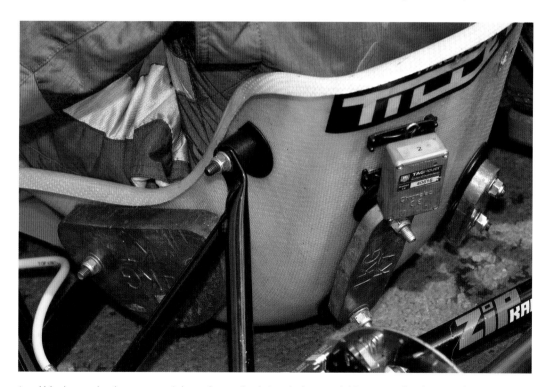

Lead blocks or other heavy material may be used to bring the kart and driver up to the class weight.

If the engine is water-cooled, is there coolant in the radiator, and is it circulating correctly without any air-locks or leaks? If there is a belt-driven water pump, are the belts in place? The fuel tank needs to be topped up and filled to approximately two-thirds of maximum.

If it is a two-stroke engine, oil will need to be mixed with the petrol, the amount determined by the type of engine and the type of oil used. Check the data sheets, or take advice from other drivers. A traditional air-cooled engine may need a ratio of sixteen parts of petrol to one part of a castor-based oil, whereas a modern water-cooled engine may need only twenty-five or even fifty to one of a synthetic oil. Always use a good quality racing oil. Measure out the desired amount in a graduated jug, then stir into a known quantity of fuel before decanting into the kart tank through a filtered funnel. Keep the funnel in a clean, sealed plastic bag so it does not become contaminated with specks of dust or dirt. So if the mixture were to be twenty-five to one, then mix 200ml of oil into 5ltr of petrol.

Take great care when mixing and decanting the fuel: consider wearing goggles and gloves, and always have a fire extinguisher to hand. Never allow petrol to fall on the tarmac as it will harm the surface, so use a mat. In hot weather fuel can vaporize and ignite easily – even a static spark from nylon clothing has been known to start a fire. Obviously do not allow anyone to smoke in the vicinity, and never mix or decant fuel in the vicinity of heaters of any type, especially space heaters. Always familiarize yourself with the location of the fire points in the paddock where the large fire extinguishers are stored. Thankfully paddock fires are rare, but if they do occur, awnings can be burnt down in a flash.

Once the fuel is in the tank, the carburettor needs to be primed. Have someone hold the throttle fully open whilst holding the other hand over the carburettor mouth, and rock the engine backwards and forwards with the rear wheel if non-clutched, or flick the starter motor on for a short burst. Alternatively remove the spark plug but keep it connected to its HT lead, and lay it on the metal part of the engine to keep it earthed, and turn the engine over more easily. This should pump the fuel through to fill the carburettor, until excess fuel is seen to be in the carburettor mouth. This procedure will make the engine fire up more quickly and easily when ready.

Running In

'Running in' is the term used in kart racing to bed in new components, and is especially applicable after fitting a new piston. If the kart's engine is brand new, or has had a major rebuild with new parts, then treat it gently to begin with. Enrich the fuel mixture by jetting higher than normal (see later in the chapter for more details about setting the jetting). Warm the engine up carefully and steadily, and never use full revs in the first session. Accelerate with full throttle and ease off, and whilst easing off choke the engine slightly to enrich the mixture to give it more lubrication. (Choking the engine is done by putting a gloved hand over the air intakes for a short time.)

Gradually increase the revs of the engine, and the length of time building up to maximum revs, until the engine is fully bedded in. With a brand new engine this could take one hour, whereas with a new piston and other parts it might take only two or three ten-minute sessions. Depending on the type of engine, it might be advisable to remove the cylinder to inspect the sides of the piston to ensure that it is wearing in evenly without showing excessive rubbing marks. More information on this issue is given in Chapter 11.

Test Sessions

Use the first couple of laps to get up to speed, then try and find clear space on the track for four or five very consistent laps. The best drivers will lap within a tenth of a second each lap. Unless you are trying to prove a setting to make the kart go faster at the end of a long race, do not spend too long pounding round and round. If there is time and a pit lane facility, come in and make a change to try the effect on lap times.

OPTIMIZING THE KART SET-UP

You will start with the standard settings recommended by the kart manufacturer, or the previous user. The kart will have been set up in the workshop so the wheels are parallel, and the same distance out on each side (as described above), then if it is dry put on about 3mm of toe-out on the front.

During practice it may be possible to come through the pit lane for some swift set-up adjustments.

Gearing

Take advice from fellow drivers for a starting point on the front and rear sprocket sizes. Some circuits will have a published list to help newcomers. So long as you have at least a basic rev-counter on the kart, preferably with a peak hold memory facility, you will be able to see the maximum rpm of the engine after a track session. Adjust the gearing so that the engine is reaching maximum rpm, and then work up and down from there in one-tooth increments. A larger rear sprocket makes for higher rpm on the engine, and a lower rear sprocket lower rpm and potentially a higher top speed if the engine has the power and torque to suit. So in the wet, when speeds will be lower, it is often advisable to use a rear sprocket with a couple of teeth more than the optimum dry setting.

Some engines may have the possibility of changing the front sprocket as well, perhaps one tooth either way from the standard sprocket. The ratio between the front and rear can be calculated, and it may be there is an overlap which gives exactly the same overall gearing. Large rear sprockets are vulnerable on kerbs, meaning the chain may be thrown off on contact, and if such large sprockets are used it may be advisable to fit a plastic sprocket guard. At some tracks there may be two completely different ratios of front to rear sprocket sizes that give very similar lap times. With a large rear sprocket the engine will rev out or over-rev on the straight, not achieving such a high top speed, but the acceleration out of the slower corners may be much better. With the small rear sprocket, the top speed on the straights may be much higher, but the kart will struggle to accelerate.

Competitors will usually have a selection of rear sprockets.

Tyre Pressures

The tyre manufacturer will usually publish their recommended tyre pressures, measured in bars or pounds per square inch. One bar is approximately 14.5psi, and most often tyre pressure gauges show both values. Generally the softer, or stickier, the tyre is, the lower the pressures used.

The manufacturer may give an optimum pressure at working temperature, so always take a measurement of all four tyre pressures as soon as the kart comes off the track, when the tyres are still hot from use. It is worth balancing the pressures side to side at this stage by initially dropping the tyre working the hardest, usually the left-hand-side tyres on a clockwise circuit, to the same reading as the other side. Then if adjustments are subsequently made, increase or decrease the pressures by the same amount.

It is also possible to use an infra-red temperature detector, or better still a probe, to check the surface temperature: in this case take three readings per tyre, the outside, middle and inside of the tread surface. These readings can give very useful information – for instance, if the middle is much hotter than the outsides, then the pressure is probably too high.

In cold weather use slightly higher tyre pressures to help the tyre come up to its working temperature; in hotter weather use lower pressures to avoid over-heating the tyre. Given the choice it is always better to use lower pressures, but the kart may be harder to drive, especially on the opening laps. If low pressures are used, ensure there are three bead pegs in the outside of the wheel rims, to prevent the bead of the tyre slipping off the rim and deflating the tyre.

Eventually the experienced mechanic or driver will be able to 'read' the surface of the tyre, and judge how well it is working. The more the tyre slides, the higher the surface temperature will become, and hence the greater the increase between the cold tyre pressure and the working tyre pressure. Some teams use dry air or even nitrogen to avoid moisture in the air used to inflate the tyre, and this reduces the increase in pressure as the tyre heats up in use. Slick kart tyres will usually be in their optimum range between 60 and 80°C; if the temperature reaches 100°C or more, blistering and failure will occur.

A mechanic checking tyre pressures.

Tyres being mounted, and a slick being prepared for balancing.

Tyre manufacturers will always recommend putting a gentle heat cycle through a set of tyres before racing for optimum extended life. But since a new tyre will often give its fastest time after two or three laps, many drivers will simply go straight out in qualifying with new tyres to get that quickest time.

Wet weather tyre pressures will usually be 50 to 100 per cent higher than the slick pressures; this keeps the blocks of the tyres stiff to displace water on the track. But as the track starts to dry, the tyre pressure should be reduced so as not to overheat the tyre. The handling of the kart will deteriorate rapidly if wet weather tyres are used on a near-dry track, and the tyres may be destroyed, so the choice of wet weather tyres or slicks at the start of a race when the track is drying is quite critical, as well as the chosen tyre pressures.

After the race or test day, wash the grit out of the tyres, deflate them, and keep them protected from sun or light in a bag. Exposure to ultra-violet light or heat will reduce the life of the tyre and harden it. They should also be kept at an even temperature of perhaps a few degrees centigrade, and never, ever allowed to be exposed to freezing temperatures, which can permanently change the structure of the tyre.

Most tyre makes are directional, and the tyre sidewall will be marked with an arrow. For slicks this is because the tyre tread is manufactured with an overlap. But at least one major manufacturer makes the tyre treads in a different way, and there is no preferred directionality. They recommend putting the logos to the outside, presumably for publicity reasons. For wet tyres the arrow is to show the direction that the tyre is designed to throw out the standing water; if used in the wrong direction, acceleration might be marginally better at the expense of braking but the tyre could aquaplane in standing water. So always use the tyre in the designated rotation.

Setting the Jetting

Optimizing the jetting, or air/fuel mixture, goes hand in hand with gearing. As you converge towards the optimum jetting and make the kart go faster, it may be possible to remove a tooth or two from the rear sprocket. Always start with a safe setting for the jets, or a larger than expected main jet.

Carburettors fall into one of two basic types: the diaphragm carburettor and the float chamber type.

Diaphragm Carburettors

Diaphragm carburettors were originally designed for chainsaws, so the engine can continue to work at any angle, even upside down. The fuel pump, pulling petrol

A diaphragm carburettor.

from the fuel tank, is built into the design and is operated by a vacuum pressure from the engine crankcase through a small pipe or hole drilled through the mounting flange. There is a high and a low jet adjuster (usually marked H and L), although some specialist carburettors may have a third jet. The jets are spring-loaded screws with a long point, and may have a washer or T-piece to make it easier to turn them whilst driving.

The point of the jet controls the amount of fuel passing down a passage into a small hole in the inside of the carburettor body. As the air rushes past it sucks the fuel into the stream of air where it is mixed, or atomized, ready to be compressed and burnt in the engine. The engine manufacturer's data sheet will give the starting points for the high and low jet settings. They are set by fully screwing the jet in, but not too tightly, then counting the turns or part turns as the screw is turned out. So a low jet might be two turns out, and a high jet perhaps half a turn out as a starting point. However, always take advice for the first time. Adjustments to the low jet will have most effect at low rpm, on acceleration, whilst adjustments on the high jet will have most effect at maximum power and rpm. As the jet is turned in, the mixture becomes leaner – but if too lean, the engine will seize up.

The amount of air flowing through the carburettor is controlled by a butterfly, or in some types a slide, which is operated by the throttle pedal connected by a cable. If the kart has such a carburettor then invest in a carburettor pressure tester, which will show the pressure reached before the carburettor 'pops' and releases the fuel. If it will not hold pressure, then it is time for a rebuild.

The cold-starting choke on a diaphragm carburettor is just a flap that restricts the amount of air entering the carburettor, operated by a small lever. There may not even be a choke, in which case the driver will put his hand over the front of the air box to restrict the air supply and make the mixture richer until the engine has started and is firing consistently.

The carburettors can be maintained quite simply by referring to the exploded diagram of parts, and carefully noting the position and orientation of each part as it is removed. Diaphragm and gasket kits are readily available. As always, it is essential to be scrupulously clean whilst stripping and rebuilding a carburettor. Carb cleaner can be used to remove any deposits, before cleaning the items in brake cleaner and re-assembling.

Do not attempt to polish or abrade any carburettor or exhaust restrictor plate as the minimum size may be exceeded, or the surface finish used to see if it has been tampered with disturbed.

Float Chamber Carburettor

As the name implies, the fuel is pumped into a float chamber and the level controlled by the floats closing or opening a cut-off valve in the fuel supply. These carburettors need a separate fuel pump, again operated by a vacuum pipe from the engine crankcase, or in some types by an actuating lever on the axle. Even though the carburettor may have a small fuel filter incorporated, it is essential to have a good quality fuel filter in the pipe from the fuel tank in all karts, and possibly remove the filter in the carburettor if the regulations allow.

A float chamber carburettor.

Competitors need to have a few spare jets, tubes and needles (when permitted in the regulations).

These carburettors have a slide and needle which simultaneously control the amount of air and fuel entering the engine. There will be jets and passages for low, mid-range and full power settings of the engine as well as the choke for cold starts, which is operated by a push-pull lever. The needle, which can be adjusted in height relative to the slide (*see* below), moves up and down in an emulsion tube, and the main jet is fixed in the bottom of the float chamber. The jets are fixed, so the mechanic has to decide before the track session which sizes to fit. Class regulations may restrict the choice of jets, needles and tubes.

There should be parts lists and exploded diagrams available on the carburettor manufacturers' websites or in their literature. The height of the floats and the fuel delivery valve are critical, so take advice for the correct measurement.

Once the optimum parts are fitted, or used according to the class regulations, the main adjustments are the size of the main jet, and the relative height of the needle. The smaller the number on the main jet, the weaker the mixture will be. The main jet is accessed by either removing the whole of the float chamber or unscrewing a large nut in the bottom of the float chamber. It can then be unscrewed and an alternative fitted. If the needle is at its lowest setting, the mixture will be weakened at low and mid-range throttle settings; if set high, then conversely the mixture will be richer at mid-range.

The needle can be accessed by unscrewing the top of the carburettor and removing the throttle cable which hooks into the top of the slide. Often a special long box spanner is required to unscrew the top of the slide to remove the needle. It has probably five notches, and a

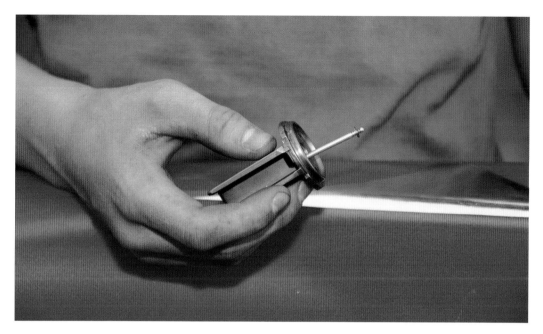

The carburettor needle is adjustable for height.

small clip and spring locates it into the slide. Having the clip in the bottom notch would be the richest position, the needle being highest. The washer can be put under or on top of the clip for finer adjustments of the needle height. There is plenty of detailed advice on settings available on websites or on manufacturers' literature.

Generally speaking, the higher the barometric pressure the smaller the main jet, or the leaner the mixture, that can be used. There are computer programs available, which can often be linked to portable weather stations, to aid the setting up of a carburettor. Humidity and air temperature also have significant effects on jetting, and changes in all of these must be taken into account. The optimum mixture for a petrol engine is called the stoichiometric ratio and is 14.7 to 1, but for a two-stroke engine with oil mixed in the fuel, the optimum ratio for maximum power is more like 12.2 to 12.5 to 1. In the future, fuel injection or electronically operated carburettors may come into use.

Always keep the carburettors spotlessly clean and free from contamination or dirt between meetings. Drain out the fuel, disposing of it safely and legally, and keep the carburettor in a clean plastic bag.

Spark Plugs

Probably it doesn't need to be said, but the spark plug plays an important role in jetting. Plugs are graded from soft to hard, or hot to cold, and there are all sorts of varieties in between. A colder plug will transfer the heat away from the working parts faster, but is more prone to fouling up; a hotter plug may over-heat too easily and cause damage to the engine. The engine manufacturer will usually recommend type numbers, perhaps from several spark plug manufacturers. If the weather is very wet or cold, it may be necessary to put in one grade hotter. Most non-American plugs use a higher number for a colder plug. 'Reading' the colour at the working end of the spark plug is the first step in determining the richness or weakness of the air/fuel mixture. The condition of the spark plug can also give vital information about the accuracy of the ignition timing.

Ignition Timing

If class regulations permit the ignition timing to be varied, take advice from the manufacturer's data sheets for an initial setting. Very often class regulations will specify a maximum advance setting. As the piston comes up to the top of the cylinder, the spark fires to ignite the mixture before it reaches the top, and gives time for the flame to reach the whole area and exert the maximum pressure at the top of the stroke. The setting is described as a number of degrees 'before top dead centre' (BTDC), or in millimetres measured in the drop of the piston from its maximum height to where the ignition fires the spark; the larger the measurement in millimetres, the more the ignition is advanced. How to set this is described in Chapter 11.

Optimizing the Jetting and Reading the Plug

To get an accurate reading of the plug colour in a two-stroke engine, the engine should ideally be switched off at maximum power after a couple of hard and fast laps, and the kart allowed to coast into the pits. If the plug is black and sooty, the mixture is too rich; if it is a dry black to light tan or grey it is correct; and if a light grey or white, the mixture is too weak.

If the engine is run for any length of time with too weak a mixture it will be in danger of seizing up because the lubrication of the piston in the cylinder will break down, and the piston will stick to the cylinder. In a light seize, maybe only the piston ring will seize and become stuck; in a heavy seize the piston will lock solid and extensive maintenance will be needed.

Detonation is another engine killer, and occurs when the last part of the mixture explodes violently rather than being burnt cleanly, causing damage to the piston and the cylinder head. Detonation can by caused by too much ignition advance, poor quality petrol, too small a squish gap (the gap between the edge of the piston and the cylinder head at top dead centre), or too lean a mixture. It may show up on the plug as tiny nodules of aluminium having been deposited from the piston, perhaps to begin with showing as small grey dots or flecks. An overall dirty grey colour also indicates too weak a mixture.

An oiled-up spark plug alongside a new replacement.

The marks on this piston show that it has seized up.

Pistons: from the left: as weak as possible, safe, slightly rich.

The next step is to examine the top of the piston, which can give an even more accurate reading of the mixture. That is best done by removing the cylinder head to expose the whole of the top of the piston, but if the engine is sealed, or time is limited, the piston can be examined through the plug hole with the aid of a bendy light. This is a tiny torch on the end of a flexible tube. Tiny video cameras can also be used on the end of a flexible lead and light.

If the piston is all black and sooty or even wet, the mixture is too rich; if light tan to pale sandy, it is near optimum; but if the top of the piston is white or grey and eroded, then it is near seizing. With older air-cooled engines a dry black might be optimum for mixture; if it is turning grey it will be too weak; and if it is showing signs of being nibbled round the edges then detonation is occurring.

If a two-stroke engine is running too rich it may four-stroke on the straights. This means that the engine is missing burning the fuel properly on each stroke, so the engine note will change and it will be felt to hold back instead of revving on cleanly. Should this happen adjust the jetting accordingly, and check again after the next session.

Compensating for Excessive Under- or Oversteer

At the same time as running on the track to adjust the jetting and gearing, the driver will be giving feedback on the kart's behaviour in the corners. Does it push on, in other words generating understeer, or is it tail happy, the back sliding out, termed oversteer: But the driver has to describe how the kart behaves on the way into the corner, what is happening in the middle of the corner, and the under- or oversteer on the way out. The aim is to have responsive steering, so the apex can be touched without the kart sliding wide, the inside rear wheel lifting off the ground just sufficiently to prevent the scrubbing action that would otherwise occur because of the lack of a differential, and to get good traction on the way out. It is very important to have neutral handling on the exit of the corner so speed is not scrubbed off by excessive under- or oversteer, thus reducing acceleration and the speed at the end of the next straight.

In Chapter 3 we saw the list of possible adjustments. Roughly speaking, the adjustments are to the width of the

Seat stays are used to stiffen the rear of the kart.

This bearing hanger has alternative ride height positions.

front or rear wheels, to the angles of the front wheels, and to stiffen or soften various parts of the chassis and its attachments. Karts have no suspension, but the whole chassis flexes, and the flex is used to adjust the amount of load transfer from rear to front. The centre of gravity therefore has a significant effect on the forces acting on the kart chassis, and may be adjusted by positioning of ballast and the height and angle of the seat. Moving weight further back will increase rear grip.

Traditionally moving the rear wheels out on the axle loses grip at the back, or moving the front wheels in, generates more oversteer. But modern chassis have a huge range of possible adjustments, so always try and record the effect for any particular kart. Once a neutral setting has been found, then move the fronts and rears in or out by the same amount to see if faster or slower times result. There is no substitute for trying an adjustment, then recording the effect. Most class regulations limit the overall width of the rear wheels to 140cm, and in the dry with a modern kart on a 40mm or 50mm diameter axle and reasonably grippy tyres the rears will usually be set near the maximum. The front is usually set some 10 to 20cm narrower. Make adjustments to width in 5mm or 10mm increments.

If the kart is understeering into the corner, try moving the fronts in. Widening the fronts will increase the flex at the front, increasing the grip in mid-corner and at the exit, but possibly at the expense of a good entry. So if the kart is understeering on the way out, move the fronts out. But working on the rear end will usually be the key to a good exit. Adding seat stays will help to stop the inside rear wheel from lifting up too high, and adding a rear torsion bar would stiffen the kart and induce oversteer.

As the track rubbers in, with more drivers leaving a rubber deposit on the racing line, it will become more grippy and it may be necessary to lose some grip from the kart so as to make it free up and exit well from corners. The rear end may start to bounce due to excess grip. The width across the rear tyres should be increased, and the fronts narrowed, or it may be necessary to reduce the rear ride height.

As the rear is widened, the axle will be able to flex more, and it is harder for the inside rear wheel to lift clear of the track. Longer hubs would make the axle stiffer. Axles come in various degrees of softness to stiffness, but it is usually best to stick with the standard axle as much as possible. A stiff rear end will make it harder to turn in when entering the corner and to hit that apex perfectly, but the inside rear wheel will return to the

A number plate is used to shield the intake box from the rain; note the rear wheels are much further in than in the dry.

ground more quickly to aid grip and acceleration on the way out of the corner.

Wet Set-up

When the track is wet and treaded tyres are mounted, the front tyres are set out to probably the greatest width possible, usually achieved by wheel rims with an offset centre and possibly by putting more spacers on the inside of the stub axles. The rear wheels are set narrower, usually achieved by using wheel rims with no offset, the mounting part of the wheel rim probably nearly central to the rim itself. Because the wet tyres are narrower, and the wheel rims also narrower to suit, it's often possible to use the same positions of the rear hubs on the axle,

otherwise the hubs may be moved in slightly. The tyre pressures are set considerably higher than for slicks, and gradually reduced if the track is starting to dry out.

The front toe-out should be increased from the normal 3mm or so to maybe as much as 10mm, and full caster applied if adjustable. Lowering the rear ride height may help the handling, as would moving the ballast higher up the seat, and even if time mounting the seat a little higher.

The air intake should be shielded from picking up water, and on gearbox karts it may be possible to reverse the intake trumpets so that they point backwards instead of forewards.

It may be worthwhile having a shield in front of the rear brake disc, and if a gearbox kart then the brake balance should be changed to have more bias towards the rear. This will help to prevent the front wheels locking up when braking.

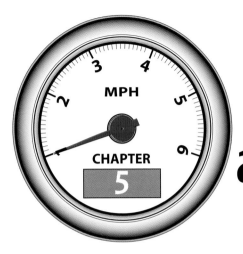

Race Tactics and Strategy

Whilst Chapter 4 described the principles of driving the racing line and basic kart set-up, and Chapter 6 sets out the timetable for a typical race day, this chapter endeavours to explore the tactics and strategies that might be employed.

SETTING UP THE KART

Weather conditions will be the first decider on how to set up the kart. Is it raining, or is the track wet or damp? In this case a wet set-up is needed, and wet weather tyres will need to be prepared and mounted. If the track is not fully wet, or the best wet weather tyres need to be preserved for later, then part-worn tyres should be used, often called 'intermediates'. Brand new wet tyres should be scrubbed in by running for a few laps on a wet track; this will remove the shiny surface on new tyres caused by the release agent from the manufacturing mould and help them to grip better when needed. However, take care to bed them in gently.

If it is hot and sunny, with high barometric pressure, then it may be possible to reduce the carburettor jetting. This is termed 'jetting down'. Conversely if it is cold with low pressure, jet up for safety until an accurate plug reading is obtained.

If there is a strong headwind on the main straight, it may be desirable to add a tooth to the rear sprocket.

If new brake pads have been fitted overnight, then use the first practice session to bed them in gently, making

Weighing the kart and driver.

sure they are not overheated. It's probably best to have fitted new engine parts and given them a run on a previous test day rather than having to run in a new piston or piston ring on the morning of a race day.

Weigh the kart before the first race with the tyres that are going to be used. Compare the weights of the slicks and wet weather tyres and wheels so if a quick change is necessary, adjustments to ballast will be known and can be quickly applied. If the difference is small, putting in more or less fuel might be all that is required – bearing in mind that a minimum of 3ltr of fuel may be required for end-of-race tests in some formulae; at any rate, never let the tank go below 1.5ltr at the end of a race. Allow at least a kilo or two in hand on weight measured with the tank at its minimum end-of-race level.

Once you are familiar with the effect of the various adjustments on the kart, it should be possible to choose how fast it starts to work optimally. This is known as 'coming on': for instance, a driver might say, 'The kart didn't come on until nearly the end of the race, and then it was too late.' It's usually best to have the kart come on at least two or three laps into the race, otherwise the handling will start to deteriorate towards the end of the race, putting the driver at risk of being overtaken. Some drivers like to have the kart work optimally straightaway so they can try and make a break, whilst others leave it until later in the race, especially if it is a long race, so they can attack at the end. The simplest way to adjust this is by altering tyre pressures: if the tyres are a little harder, the kart will come on quickly, but if the pressures are a little reduced from normal, the kart will come on later when the tyres come fully up to temperature.

The decision on this strategy will be affected by whether the driver is at the front or back of the grid.

OVERTAKING AND DEFENDING

There is nothing like the thrill of making a good pass on another competitor, unless it is winning the race itself. If the two karts are fairly evenly matched, then a clean pass is not easy, but it is possible. The most important factors are to be decisive but not over-ambitious. If the kart lacks a little pace, perhaps at the beginning of a race when it is set to come on at the end, then it is important to defend: never give up a place unless with good reason and a clear strategy.

A good overtaking move, where the overtaking driver has claimed the apex.

Overtaking

The MSA's 'Blue Book' has some important advice:

> Overtaking, according to the circumstances, may be carried out either on the right or on the left. However, manoeuvres liable to hinder other drivers, such as more than one change of direction to defend a position, deliberate crowding of a car beyond the edge of the track, or any other abnormal change of direction, are strictly prohibited. Any driver who appears guilty of any of the above offences may be reported to the Clerk of the Course.

Either you have caught another driver, in which case you must be the faster, or you are stuck behind another driver for a number of laps. In the first instance it is important to strike immediately while you have the momentum of being faster, and possibly also taking the other driver by surprise. The most likely place to overtake in this circumstance is by outbraking them into a corner. Always be planning ahead, thinking several corners or even laps ahead so you have a good plan in mind when you catch the other competitor. Watch the other races, especially the experienced drivers at the front, to see where they make their overtaking moves. You can never stop learning!

If you are following another driver you will be looking to see where you might be a little faster, and where they have the edge, and simultaneously putting pressure on, hoping they will make a mistake. But don't make it obvious to the other driver *where* you are faster, as they will use the information to defend more at that point. If they do make a mistake, be ready to pounce. If the mistake is in a corner, you may be able to get a better exit and roar past on the way out. Look to get to the side where the next corner turns in your favour.

Overtaking on the exit of a corner.

Outbraking a rival for a good overtake.

So the two most common overtakes are outbraking into a corner, or accelerating out faster. In the first instance you will need to be faster down the straight and later on the brakes. That means getting a perfect exit from the preceding corner and using as much of the slip-stream as possible for a tow, then darting out at the last moment to outbrake your rival. Slipstreaming and the art of getting a tow from the preceding kart is using the effect of the kart in front as it punches a hole in the air, leaving behind a partial vacuum. Your kart is placed in this vacuum, so less power is needed from your engine for the same speed, and when you dart out your momentum will give you a temporary higher top speed. Slipstreaming works best on a long straight followed by a medium corner – but remember, if it is easy for you to slipstream and pass, then it will also be easy for your rival to regain the place on the next lap.

If this move is for a win, then it could be worth considering waiting for the last lap, remembering that your rival will be ready and will try and block the move. As you start to get alongside, your rival will try and turn in, and if contact is made then you might both spin out. This is one

of the most common reasons for a crash, neither kart giving way. Being decisive and getting your kart fully alongside is the key. Then let your kart run out to the edge of the track, blocking any attempt to re-pass, but obviously without trying to run your competitor off the track. Sometimes in a slower corner, if you are just ahead on the apex, it is worth just slowing the pace slightly to prevent the rival from picking up his speed and coming back at you later. If you were second in a queue of karts, and manage to put the leader on the outside, the chances are that the third-placed driver will be able to sneak inside the erstwhile leader as well. If they then start fighting, it might give you a chance to pull away.

Usually the outbraking is done on the inside of a corner, but sometimes it is possible to outbrake a driver round the outside. The corner needs to have good grip on the outside, and good run-off in case the rival can just come back across and block the move – but if the next corner turns the opposite way and you can get alongside, the move might be worthwhile. An opportunity like this might present itself if the rival has been taking an exceptionally tight line to defend the inside.

Risky but successful overtaking on the outside.

Whether you decide to go for the inside or the outside, check out the condition of the track on the previous lap for dust and marbles (tyre debris) or damp patches, as well as carefully checking kerb edgings.

Almost every pass will have been set up one or more corners ahead. You are trying for a faster exit speed on the preceding corner, so it might even have been worthwhile dropping back a fraction to get a run out of a corner in order to have the momentum to pass. In any case, slow in and fast out is well known to give faster lap times, and may allow you to draw alongside on the following straight. If you are putting pressure on a driver hoping for a mistake, position your kart differently on consecutive laps so they are never sure where you might attack. If they look round to see where you are, put your kart in their blind spot so they can never be sure where you are. Remember that as the race progresses they may start to make more mistakes as they tire, so if you are consistent,

alert and keep up the concentration you will have the edge. Common mistakes are outbraking themselves, missing the apex, running too wide on the way out, or missing a gear. Bear in mind that if you are in a queue of karts, the one behind you will also be looking for any chance of an opening.

A chance to overtake might present if the leader is coming up to lap a back-marker. The rival may hesitate for a fraction, or choose the wrong side of

the back-marker to pass, in which case you will be ready to pounce.

So long as you are confident on cold tyres at the start of a race, you may be able to pick off other drivers who are less confident. Alternatively if there is a queue into a corner it may give the opportunity for a risky move round the outside. Always remember with a pass into a corner, that the other driver may get you back on the way out if your line has been compromised; this is commonly known as the 'switchback'.

Making the most of the queues at the start of a race.

Defending

The chances are that you will do just as much defending as attacking. Remembering the advice in the 'Blue Book' about track etiquette, you can legally make one move to block or defend. So, knowing your weak points on the track, position the kart for maximum defence where you are weakest. Thus if you are slow on the straights relative to the pursuer, but faster in the corners, concentrate on getting through the twisty parts and getting a good exit. Conversely if you go too fast into the corner because of the pressure, and overshoot the apex, you will be very exposed on the way out or on the following straight. Don't look behind! Looking behind is the first sign of weakness and will easily be picked up by your rival. You will hear the kart behind, and can figure out its position.

One tactic that some drivers adopt is to back the rival into the next chasing group: just slightly ease the pace in the hope that your rival will come under attack from the following drivers and let you escape. However, this is a dangerous tactic at the end of the race as each of them will see a chance for victory, and fight furiously to get to the front. So sometimes the wisest tactic is to let the rival past and settle the fight later in the race.

Working with Another Driver

If two, three or four drivers can break away at the start, then rather than fight amongst themselves, the best plan might be to work together to keep clear and extend the gap from the chasing group. Leave the fight for late on in the race. The other benefit is that it gives you time to size up the other drivers' weak and strong points, and also passes the advantage to you if your kart is set up to be strong at the end. However, if there are just two karts in

Defending hard on the last lap.

Breaking away in a small group.

the breakaway, and you sense someone approaching, the best plan might be to overtake and leave your rival to fight, rather than risk someone else joining in.

The other time it can be worthwhile working with another driver is during timed qualifying. The key factor here is to get a good tow down the main straight, and with the other driver's co-operation, to come out and pass with higher than normal speed just before the timing line.

RECOVERING FROM AN INCIDENT

At some time or another you are bound to crash, or at least stop on the track, either because you have made a driving error, or someone else has, or there has been a mechanical failure. The error might result in a simple spin with no contact and the chance to recover and get back into the race with a minimum loss of time, or it might mean a race-ending crash against a barrier – although this is more likely the result of contact or mechanical failure.

This is where the driver's protective clothing comes into full effect. Karts have no seatbelts, so most drivers would brace their arms against the steering wheel. Depending on the severity of the contact, the driver might be lifted out of the seat and fall back in, or be totally ejected, relying on their suit and helmet for protection.

In race cars with seatbelts the advice to the driver is always to remove the hands from the steering wheel, as the greatest risk is sustaining a broken wrist or hand from the wheel whipping round violently as the front

Crashes do sometimes happen, but no one was injured in this spectacular incident.

Safety gear protects the driver if he is ejected from the seat.

wheels impact with the barrier. If the impact is very severe in a kart, there is also the chance of the steering wheel impacting on the driver's chest, so a rib protector should be considered. If the kart is obviously going no further, the priority is for the driver to get to a place of safety, and also if it is possible and safe to move the kart to a safer place. The driver should immediately raise his hand to warn other drivers of the incident.

If the kart is spinning, then stop as soon as possible by pressing the brake, and do not let the kart roll back into the path of following karts. If the kart is stationary the following drivers will be able to take evasive action, but if the kart is still spinning sometimes the advice is for the following drivers to aim for the kart, on the assumption that by the time their kart arrives at the spot the spinning kart will have moved elsewhere. But remember that karts stop very quickly, unlike spinning race cars.

If you are spinning on your own too often, perhaps you are overdriving, so you need to think carefully about this after the race. In any case the Clerk of the Course will not think very highly of anyone who is consistently proving to be a risk to others.

Quick Action Needed

Every second stopped, spinning or recovering is a second lost in the race, and assuming that the kart is not damaged, the priority is to get back into the race as soon as possible. Do not waste time cursing the driver who took you off, leave that for your complaint to the Clerk of the Course after the race. If the kart has a self starter and the engine has stopped, fire it up and re-join when safe to do so. If the kart has no clutch, then you will have to jump out to push-start it yourself.

It is essential to warn other drivers if you have a problem.

Pull the kart to a safe place if you can.

After a crash, the priority is to get back in the race if possible.

This is worth practising on your own so that the technique comes naturally in an emergency. For Cadet and Junior races, incident marshals may be allowed on track to help restart karts, but their priority will be the safety of the driver. If it is a gearbox kart with a clutch, then if possible the clutch will have been grabbed at the start of the incident in the hope of keeping the engine running.

Forced off the Track

If you are forced wide and find yourself driving outside the perimeter of the track, perhaps because another driver has forced you wide or you have made an error, it is important to gently ease the kart back safely. Make the smallest possible steering movements, and if the kart is on a slippery surface such as grass, do not hit the brakes.

Ease back on the throttle and look to find a gap in the traffic to rejoin the race. If you find yourself on run-off tarmac which affords good grip, then of course stamp on the brakes if necessary to avoid contact. Some corners may have an escape route, and this is something you should have checked during your track walk earlier. But if you take a short cut without stopping you may later be penalized, even up to a lap, so try to avoid that.

Injury

Thankfully injuries are rare in kart racing, though they do happen occasionally. Should you be injured, or trapped in the kart, do not panic, as help will be on its way instantly: every race run under an MSA permit will have an ambulance and a licensed paramedic or doctor. Raise

Practice Starts and Adjustments

In case of the engine stalling after an incident or spin, it is as well to practise starting the kart on your own. This is relatively easy if the engine is the TAG type with an electric start button, but harder if you have to get out and push. Make sure there is no approaching traffic, or start in a run-off area. Put one hand on the steering wheel and the other on the back of the seat to pull and just lift the kart off the rear wheels until enough speed is reached to be able to drop the kart, jump in and get the right leg on to the throttle.

If it is a gearbox kart, put the engine in neutral. The rear wheels will not need to be lifted, so when enough speed is reached, jump in, bang it into first or second gear and slightly open the throttle.

Also practise reaching for all the controls so that it becomes second nature without looking. Make sure you can reach the choke, carburettor adjustment screws and any radiator cooling flap as well as the obvious controls.

Push-starting a direct-drive kart after a spin.

Mechanical failure pit for repairs.

your hand if you can. The paramedics will be very careful if there is any suspicion of a neck or back injury, and will almost certainly put you in a back board; however, probably this will be just a precaution until a full assessment has taken place. Depending on the extent of any suspected injury they may ask you to be taken to hospital by a friend, or arrange for you to be taken to the Accident and Emergency department without delay.

On the other hand, if after assessment they clear you to race, you may even be able to rejoin at the back of the race if it had been stopped, so long as you and your kart have been passed as safe.

Kart clubs, like any business, will have to complete an accident book with details, and if a driver's limb was broken, or an overnight stay in hospital has been necessary, then they will have to make a special report called a RIDDOR report. So they may follow up with a phone call the following day for more details.

Pitting for Repairs

If your kart has a mechanical defect which the organizers deem unsafe to yourself or other competitors, or it renders your kart ineligible, then you may receive the mechanical failure flag. This is a black flag with an orange disc and will be displayed along with the competition number of the kart in question. The driver needs to pit within the next lap for repairs or retirement.

Most, but not all circuits have a pit entrance and a means of returning to the track after repairs. Make sure you are familiar with the procedures at each race circuit. It might be possible to repair the kart and return to the race, rejoining with care and looking for a gap in the traffic. You may have a mechanic ready with, for instance, a spare front fairing. However, remember that in all likelihood a scrutineer will want to inspect your kart before you rejoin. But if a repair is not possible, do not despair, as in most cases you will still be awarded a place in the race results based on the number of laps completed.

THE DASH FOR THE CHEQUER

Many drivers start to defend their position too vigorously and too early, slowing themselves and their rival, and allowing others to catch up. However, it is essential not to

offer an opening on the last few corners on the last lap, so keep tight lines without overly slowing the pace so much that a rival could drive round the outside, or get a much better exit from a corner. The route to the finish line might well be modified on the last lap to prevent another driver taking a shorter line to the chequer.

Once past the chequered flag, slow down gradually and safely to make your way to the weighing in and *parc fermé* area. Raise your arm as you approach the track exit. Be careful not to overtake any karts that are still on their last racing lap, and do not overtake any karts between the finish line and the track exit as that will be subject to yellow flag rules.

Post Race

If you have been good enough to win, there will be handshakes, perhaps even some hugs, and immense pleasure. However, make sure not to make any elementary errors whilst weighing in and scrutineering. Do not on any account accept anything from anyone, especially liquids, until you have been weighed, and do not leave the scrutineering area until you are sure you have permission from the Chief Scrutineer.

Protect your line to the finish without losing speed.

Celebrations after the race.

The clerk of the course may hold an inquiry into an incident.

Television and newspaper reporters may want a word or two.

Do not remove your kart unless you are sure permission has been given. There may be eligibility checks on your kart and engine, so you may have to fetch tools in order to strip down parts under the direction of the scrutineers. They are not permitted to dismantle parts themselves, but you can nominate a mechanic to do so on your behalf. However, if anything untoward is found, then you will have to present yourself, with your guardian if you are under eighteen years of age, firstly to the Chief Scrutineer to hear the objection, and if you wish to sign the forms, and then to be interviewed by the Clerk of the Course. Only the Clerk of the Course can issue a penalty: the scrutineer reports the facts.

If you disagree with the findings you may be able to appeal the severity of the penalty at the time, but the Clerk will not be deemed competent to decide on the merits or otherwise of a technical dispute. If you wish to object to the eligibility decision you will have to appeal to the Motor Sports Council, and they will hold an Eligibility Appeal Panel hearing (EAP).

Should you find yourself being sent to the Clerk of the Course for an on-track incident, then be calm and collected. Be sure to put your side of the story clearly and effectively, and try and find a witness who will support your version.

Whatever you do, never enter a discussion with a driver with whom you have had an on-track incident prior to the clerk's hearing. Words can become heated, or the argument even come to blows, either of which will land one or both drivers in very serious trouble, probably resulting in a large fine and the possible withdrawal of the racing licence, and maybe referral to the Motor Sports Council for further action.

Interviews

If you are lucky enough to be interviewed by a journalist or a television crew, be concise, be articulate, and if possible thank your team and sponsors. Do not start blaming others. Tell the story of your race, and try and give some good, sound insights as to the crucial moves you made. Now is the time for a coffee or energy drink, to help you through the interviews and podium or prize-giving process.

MPH

CHAPTER

6

A Typical Race Day

ENTERING A RACE

Now it's time to enter a race. You will have chosen and joined a club and received your club membership card, passed your ARKS novice driver test and received your competition licence from the MSA. Of course, if you have decided to race at a non-MSA approved race meeting, you will not need a licence, but you may have to prove your competency to the organizers in some other way. Remember that if you are under eighteen years of age, and do not need a medical examination by a doctor because you have been able to self-declare all the medical requirements, you can use the licence application form in lieu of a licence for the first race only.

Your club may have sent you a pack of entry forms, but if they have not, ask for one, or download one from the club's website. The club may even offer on-line entry procedures. Put the entry in a couple of weeks before the race; most club meetings close their entries a week before, and most big championships two weeks before. Some take late entries at an extra fee. Let's have a look at the sequence of events.

Filling in the Entry Form

Most club entry forms require the same basic information: the date of the meeting, and your name, address, post code, telephone number and email address. The town or city that you use in your address will be printed in the programme, then there will be a space for your competition number. Maybe your club issued you a previously unused number when you joined; if so, use that. If you go to another club meeting, that number may not be free, so the competition secretary will issue you something similar.

If you put in a stamped addressed envelope for acknowledgement of the entry, they will probably confirm the number you will use, or you may get an acknowledgement email confirmation. Numbers from one to fifteen (one to nine in gearbox classes) are used by the top finishers in the national championships and 0 (zero) for the O Plate national championship winner, so these are not available. This might change to one to ten for all classes, leaving eleven to ninety-nine available. The maximum number normally allowed is ninety-nine. Remember that as a novice, you will have to use black number plates with white numbers, then after your five signatures you can change to the normal class colours. Tick the 'Novice' box to show that you are still a novice, if appropriate.

Put down your licence number; if it hasn't come through yet, then put TBA, and tick the box for the appropriate grade. If you are in a team, or have a parent or guardian with an entrant's licence, put down that number too, otherwise leave it blank. If you have purchased a transponder for the race timing, put down the number in the box provided. If you need to hire a transponder from the club, add a suitable note so they are aware of this.

Officials at a kart race meeting

MSA Steward
Responsible on behalf of the MSA for the proper running of the meeting, second judicial body assisted by two club stewards

Clerk of the Course (assisted by Deputy & Assistant Clerk of the Course)
Overall responsiblity for the control of the event

Off-track	Technical	On-track
Secretary of the Meeting (Competition Secretary)	Chief Scrutineer	Chief Marshal
Timekeepers	Eligibility Scrutineer	Observers
Lap-Scorers	Scrutineers	Flag & Incident Marshals
Results Team	Environmental Scrutineer (Noise checks)	Starter
		Grid Marshal
		Paramedic or Doctor Medical team

Entries CLOSE Saturday 1 week prior to event

SHENINGTON KART RACING CLUB LTD

Sonja Game, Competition Secretary, 16 Graham Road, Bicester, Oxon OX26 2HP
Tel 01869 320157   Fax 01869 247981   Email skrc-compsec@hotmail.co.uk

DATE OF MEETING:	/	/	2011

Class:		Race No:	
First Name:		Surname:	

Transponder Number:	Txp								

Chassis:		Novice:	Yes No
Engine:		Licence No:	
Club:		Licence Type:	A C B B(Novice)
Entrant:		Entrants Licence No:	
Your Address:			
Town:		Post Code:	
Tel No:		Email: enables automatic confirmation	

Name of person to contact in case of Emergency:

Post Code:		Tel No:	

Held under the General Regulations of The Motor Sports Association (incorporating the provisions of the International Sporting Code of the FIA) and the Supplementary Regulations.

NOTE: W   P / /

Signed:

Name:

Address:

Signed:

Date: Age if under 18 yrs:

Entry Fee: Members £45   Non Members £55   TKM Clubman(inc.Sat pm) Fee £60   Late Entry Fee £10
Please choose your payment method for the following amount:
I wish to pay by cheque
Please make your cheque payable to SKRC Ltd, write your name, class and race number on the reverse and enclose with entry form.

Driver details will be held on a Database and will be subject to the provisions of the Data Protection Act 1998.

SKRC LTD COMPANY – VAT REGISTERED No. 770041854
www.sheningtonkrc.co.uk

Office Use ONLY:
Date Received:_____

Race entry form.

The transponder is used for electronic timing and fits on the back of the seat.

You need to put down the make of your kart, for example Tonykart, and the make of the engine, for example Rotax, and the name of your club. This will all be printed in the programme, so please make it legible. The club name will probably be abbreviated in the programme, for example 'SKRC' for 'Shenington Kart Racing Club'. If you are a member of the club where you are entering, then put down that club name, otherwise put down your 'home' club.

It is necessary to give the name and telephone number of a person to contact in an emergency in the unlikely event that you are taken to hospital – this could be of your partner, another friend, or a parent or guardian. If you are under eighteen years of age you need to state your age and put down your parent or guardian's name and address, and they must also sign the form, as well as yourself, and provide a PG Entrant licence.

For payment the traditional method was by cheque, but more and more clubs are now taking credit or debit cards, sometimes with a small surcharge. If it is a late entry you may be able to pay on the day, but if you don't turn up, don't expect any favours next time. If you need to withdraw your entry, let the club know as soon as possible; depending on the notice given, there may be a deduction from your refund.

Checklist: What to Take to the Track

- Kart
- Engine
- Spare engine
- Slick tyres and wheels
- Wet weather tyres and wheels
- Fuel for the kart
- Two-stroke racing oil to mix with the fuel (if a two-stroke engine)
- Measuring jug for the oil and mixing container for the fuel
- Toolbox with appropriate spanners, screwdrivers and sockets
- Foot pump or air compressor
- Tyre pressure gauge
- Chain spray
- Hydraulic brake fluid
- Cleaning fluid
- Kart trolley
- Kart cover to protect it from rain or strong sun
- Competition licence/PG Entrant licence if under 18
- Club membership card
- Rulebooks – *Kart Race Yearbook* and MSA 'Blue Book'
- Logbook for your engine(s) if applicable
- Homologation papers for your kart and engine (if appropriate)
- Money for incidentals and emergency spares
- Kart race suit
- Race boots
- Race gloves
- Crash helmet
- Spare tinted visor for sunny weather
- Demister spray for helmet visor
- Race wetsuit
- Food and drink
- Rags for cleaning the kart
- Spare sprockets for the gearing
- Spare battery for the kart (if appropriate) and/ or charger
- Spare spark plug, chain, sprockets, nuts and bolts
- Notebook to jot down your settings, or refer to earlier tests

Grades of Meeting

Just like competitor licence grades, events are also graded. As a novice you would be able to enter a Clubman or National B event (so long as the regulations do not exclude novices) but not a National A event. Clubman events are open to up to fifteen invited clubs, National B to invited associations, and National A usually to all drivers unless otherwise specified. National A graded events are usually just for major championships.

PREPARING FOR RACE DAY

It's always best to prepare in advance for the day of your entered race. For instance, it is advisable to fill up your fuel cans in advance so you don't need to stop on the way to the track. Pack your race suit, gloves, boots and helmet in a bag, and most importantly, don't forget your race competition licence: if you don't have it with you, at best there will be a fee to pay, at worst you may not be allowed to race.

If you are not sure of the route to the track, print out the directions, noting the post code and the circuit telephone number so you can inform them if you are delayed. Read through the club's supplementary regulations, and if you are a member, the club's championship regulations. There may be restrictions at the track, such as non-permitted areas, or a ban on pets, that you should be aware of in advance. If you passed your medical wearing spectacles or contact lenses, make sure you wear them for racing. If you haven't been before, try and find out in advance the best gearing for your kart. Sometimes the club will publish recommended starting points, otherwise another racer or the local kart shop may be able to help. Fit the recommended gearing before you leave. If you are not familiar with the track, download a map of the circuit or look at it on Google Earth, and learn the layout in advance. If you are under eighteen years of age and your parent or legal guardian is not coming, you will need a standard letter from them to give permission to whoever is signing you on for the day, to show to the club officials.

In most cases you will be able to buy spares at the circuit, but don't rely on it.

Travelling shops are usually available at the trackside.

PROCEDURE BEFORE RACING

On arrival at the circuit you will need to find somewhere to park for the day. At many tracks regular racers may have booked annual pit spaces, and visitors can sometimes book one just for the weekend, but you would need to do this in advance. The advantage is you have a guaranteed spot to park in, and probably nearer the dummy grid and facilities than if you leave it to chance. If you don't have such a space, make sure you don't inadvertently park in someone else's spot: these allocated spaces will be marked out with numbers, but if in doubt ask a club official for advice on parking. Get set up, put up your tent or awning if you have one, and get the kart ready.

Go and sign on at race control, take your licence and club membership card, plus any outstanding fees payable. You will be given a race programme and a scrutineering card. If you have forgotten your licence the MSA steward will need to be convinced that you actually hold one, and there will be a fine to pay. You could use previous race results to convince the steward of your eligibility. Carefully observe the time schedule in the programme.

Take your licence and membership card to sign on.

The Safety Scrutineering Procedure

Next you need to get your kart and racewear in the queue for safety scrutineering. Fill in the scrutineering card with your name, class, competition number, make of kart and chassis number, make of engine and engine number. If you have a spare engine, put in its make and engine number as well, and if you are in a class where a sealed engine is mandatory, put down the seal numbers.

It's very important to put down these numbers accurately because they could be checked at any time by the scrutineers, and if they don't match the numbers on your kart you could be excluded. The reason is to limit the number of kart chassis and engines available to a driver during the day, for economy reasons. If you wreck your kart you may be able to use a spare one, but the scrutineers will want to keep your original until the end of the day, and you will have to ask their permission. So ask someone else to check that you have written down the numbers correctly, and then sign the form. If you are under eighteen years of age, your parent or guardian for the day or the team entrant must sign it as well.

The main purpose of scrutineering at this stage is to check that your kart is safe to race, and that all your race wear is legal for racing. If any part of your race wear is not valid, the scrutineers will keep it for the rest of the day so it cannot be used, and you will have to find an alternative to show them; you can retrieve your own after your last race. For instance, your helmet needs an MSA sticker on the right-hand side before you can race: there is a small fee for checking the helmet and affixing the sticker, but once done, it can last for the life of the helmet. The scrutineers will make sure there are no holes in your gloves or in your boots, as the holes may catch in the pedals. Ideally you should be wearing your race suit, so they can check it fits properly.

Next the scrutineers will check the kart, first for safety. The main areas checked include the operation of the brake, to ensure that the brake pedal does not come over the front bumper when pushed down; that the wheel nuts are of a locking type; and that the wheels are fitted properly. Any ballast needs to be safely fitted, with a minimum of two fasteners and no more than 5kg on any one place. They will look to see if a steering column collar is fitted, that the lock nuts are all tight and showing at least one thread above the nut, and that the bodywork is securely fitted. They will make sure that catch tanks are fitted to the fuel tank overflow, and to any oil vents in the engine or gearbox. There should not be any projections underneath the kart, because these could be a hazard if it over-rides another machine.

Scrutineers will check your kart and race wear for compliance with regulations.

A clutch guard and chain guard are mandatory.

Clutch and chain guards will also be on their list of checks, and they will want to see that the exhaust and any other parts, including the seat, are fitted safely and securely.

At this point they may not be checking all the detailed measurements to ensure that your kart meets the regulations, but if they spot something they will let you know. Listen carefully to any suggestions for improvement, or requirements for change before racing. Never argue with a scrutineer, be polite, and they will help you to the best of their ability. If something needs doing, ask if they need to see the kart again after it is fixed. Sometimes the tyres get marked for the day at this stage, sometimes it is done later. Most clubs only allow you to use one set of slicks for the whole day, again to save costs, and you should check if you need to use these tyres during the practice period or not. If in doubt, use the ones you plan to race with.

Different clubs have different methods of confirming you have had your kart scrutineered. Some might tick you off on a list, some might put a sticker or even a seal on the kart.

Now that you are all ready for practice, are fully safety scrutineered, and hopefully have a little time to spare before the drivers' briefing, it might be a good time to walk the track. If possible walk round the whole track, taking note of the marshal post positions, any run-off areas, and where you exit the track.

RACE DAY FORMAT

Don't be late for the drivers' briefing, or you could be fined; the official time will be in your programme, but listen out for tannoy announcements as well. Very often novices and first timers at the track will be asked to stay behind for an extra briefing, so don't hesitate to ask a question if in doubt about anything. The Clerk of the Course will hold the briefing, and run over anything particular they want to bring to drivers' attention. They may emphasize how they want to see the race starting procedure: listen carefully about what to do should there be a false start, and where to stop if there is a red flag. Familiarize yourself with the officials running the meeting: their names will be printed in the programme, and try and match the names to faces so you know who's who. The Chief Clerk of the Course runs the meeting.

The drivers' briefing is often held outside.

Note the position of the environmental scrutineer, whose task is to check the noise level of every kart as it passes beneath the microphone: if a kart is just slightly above the noise limit, a verbal or written improvement order may be issued, but if it is substantially above the limit, it will be flagged in. The other duty of the environmental scrutineer is to check that all competitors have a fire extinguisher of regulation size in their pit area.

The Practice Laps

By now your kart should be all ready, fuelled up, and with tyres mounted that are suitable for the weather and properly pressured. Check the programme for the order of practice, but don't go down to the grid too early, as you will just cause congestion. On the other hand, on no account miss the three laps of practice, as it is a requirement to allow you to race. If you do miss your turn, go and see the Clerk of the Course immediately to see if he will let you go out later.

The practice is also a good chance to make sure your kart is working properly, and helps you to dial it in for the forthcoming race. If you haven't already done so, take the opportunity to check the weight of your kart and yourself, to ensure you are within the limits allowed for the class.

> **FACT**
>
> **Typical Race Day Programme**
>
> **0800–0900:** Signing on
> **0800–0915:** Scrutineering
> **0930:** Drivers' briefing
> **0945:** Three laps practice in class race order
> **1030:** Heats – two or three for each driver
> **1500 approximately:** Lunch break
> **1530:** Start of finals
> **1800, or thirty minutes after the last race result:** Prize-giving

Although the scales will have a certificate to ensure accuracy, something may have changed since your last event, so never take the weight for granted, always check.

Preparing for the First Heat

After the practice laps you will have time to make any adjustments, which you think might make the kart go faster. Take the time before the first heat for a thorough check of

Check the noticeboard for your results.

all the nuts and bolts, and check your tyre pressures again before you go out; as a novice you will be starting from the back. Your position on the grid for the heats may be in the programme or posted on the noticeboard, but if there are last-minute entries or withdrawals it could have changed, and you might even be in a different heat to what you thought – so always check the noticeboard.

Instead of a heat, some clubs might have a timed practice period, in which case novices earn their race position on merit and do not need to start at the back. The number of karts permitted in a race is set down on the track licence, but clubs may voluntarily further reduce the number; however, they may not go above the track licence limit. Most tracks are permitted about thirty karts in a race.

When the time approaches for your first heat, take the kart up to the dummy grid ready to move into place when the race before yours goes out. If the weather is changeable, you may need to carry out a last-minute change of tyres from slick to wet, or vice versa. Take the alternative tyres with you, and enough tools to effect the changeover, and make any other adjustments to the kart that are necessary or desirable. Some kart trolleys have spikes to hold the spare tyres, or you could hang your tyre bag from the trolley.

Make sure you have some extra pressure in the tyres – you can always reduce the pressures on the grid, so take along a gauge. If a last-minute change is necessary, changing the wheels is the priority; after that there may be time to alter other settings, such as turning the airbox round or shielding it from spray. The organizers will not wait for you, so it is essential that you make that sort of decision in plenty of time.

Also be sure that you have observed the basic dimensions, such as the overall width of the kart not exceeding 1,400mm, and sidepods inside the tyres if applicable. You may also need to change your visor from tinted to clear, or put on a wetsuit.

Put the kart down on the dummy grid on the number equivalent to your starting position, but be prepared to move if someone doesn't turn up on time. If there are no numbers painted on the ground, estimate the position. You or your mechanic then needs to take your trolley to the trolley park, near the exit from the track. Put on your helmet and gloves and prepare for the race. Be aware that other drivers may try to distract you on the dummy grid, playing mind games – so look cool and confident

Take your kart to the grid in plenty of time for each race.

If the weather is changeable, take the spare tyres with you.

Novices have black number plates and start at the back of the heat grids.

while waiting to go out, and do not show any signs of weakness in attitude or words.

Have an arrangement with your mechanic to give hand signals to show if a kart is closing on you, or whether you have plenty of space behind.

The Race

Sit in the kart and mentally prepare for the race. Visualize the formation lap, and decide where you can 'lean' on the tyres to warm them up without excessive weaving, which would earn you a penalty. Hopefully you will have watched some earlier races, and seen where the poleman generally slows down the pack for the starting speed.

When this happens, be careful not to get caught out and run into the back of the kart in front. Memorize the numbers of the karts in front and to the side of you, so that if you lose or gain position on the formation lap you know where to get back to before the start. If you are in a gearbox kart where there will be a standing start, make sure you know the start grid number, and if there is more than one formation lap look for your position on the first

pass. Remember that many gearbox grids will be a 3–2–3 formation rather than the 2 x 2 formation rolling start.

Finally visualize the start of the race, mentally preparing for the rush when the start red light goes out and the green comes on, and what your plan is for the first corner.

When the grid is given the green flag to move on to the track, be careful not to skid wide at the first corner on cold tyres – this is a sure way to raise a laugh from the onlookers. Warm the tyres as much as possible with some acceleration on the corners and firm braking, then settle into the formation speed coming up to the start line.

Watch the lights, but be aware that if they fail, the starter may drop the national flag. Alternatively he may wave the karts round for a second formation lap, and show the false start flag. If the race has a false start, the next marshal post will also display the false start chevron.

At some tracks the karts will be waved through a cut-through to save time, so be ready to slow down for this. In most cases the signal to start racing will be when the red light goes out, rather than when the green light comes on, but watch previous races to check how it is done.

Karts line up in grid formation for the rolling start.

Gearbox karts usually have a standing start.

The green light coming on, or the red going out, means go.

A false start is indicated by a green flag with a yellow chevron.

If the start is good, fight for your position into the first corner, but remember the old adage that races cannot be won here, but can easily be lost. If you are on the outside you will generally want to slot into the inside line as soon as possible. Sometimes running round the outside of the other karts is an option, but it is a risky one should someone spin out and catch you.

The start is probably the riskiest part of the whole race, so it is important to be firm but fair with other competitors. Look for passing opportunities at the next few corners, and settle into a race pace. Concentrate hard, and look out for flag signals, especially yellow flags when no overtaking is allowed. If there has been a serious incident the yellow and black quarter flags may be deployed, in which case the whole pack needs to slow down behind the leader at formation lap speed, with no overtaking. Watch out for on-track hazards, and for the green flag displayed at the start line, which means the race is back on.

Remember that racing calls for a very high level of concentration, where everything else must be excluded from your mind: it is very different to driving a road car.

If the red flags are displayed, all karts must slow and stop at the spot designated by the officials.

Red Flag Stoppage

If the red flag is deployed, slow down and drive carefully to the place indicated by officials to stop. If the track is blocked and you cannot drive past the incident you should be allowed your position back on the restart; if, however, you are part of the incident, you may be allowed to start at the back so long as your kart has been inspected and passed by the scrutineer, and you have been assessed as fit by the medics.

No work is allowed on the kart during the red flag incident unless all karts are sent back to the paddock to have their race later on. Sometimes permission is given to change spark plugs, but that will be all. If your kart needs work you will have to wait for the restart, then go into the pits for repairs before rejoining the race; this is so that those who have incurred damaged do not get an unfair advantage over those that have managed to avoid incidents. If a kart has stopped or retired before the incident causing the red flag stoppage, it will not normally be allowed a restart; however, it is always worth asking politely.

Before the restart the karts will need to be assembled in grid order if a complete new race is going to take

Ambulances and paramedics will be on hand for any serious incident.

place, or in single-file race order if the race is well under way. Be ready to push your kart to the required position, remembering there will probably be a number of missing karts. If the grid is assembled in single file, the green flag will be waved at the end of the first formation lap to restart the race. Be ready, and don't leave any big gaps between your kart and the one in front.

Making up Places

Push hard either to close the gap to the kart ahead, or to look for an opening where a safe pass is possible. Be aware that others behind you will be doing the same, so don't turn in on a passing kart and perhaps take both of you off the track – but don't make it too easy, either. Should you lose a place, try and keep up with the kart ahead: often they can 'tow' you up to the next bunch.

When you start to pressurize a kart in front, or have just been passed, the other driver may give a signal indicating that he wants to work together with you to move forwards. You must make the judgement whether to do this, and perhaps get up to the next karts, or fight past and take the risk you will both lose time. Watch out for the last lap board, but don't assume it will be shown. Other drivers will be doing their utmost to make a move before the finish, and so should you, though without excessive risk, of course.

Once past the chequered flag, slow down and raise an arm as you exit the track at a safe speed. You may be picked out for weighing at the end of the race, so wait patiently in line – and never, ever, succumb to the temptation of accepting a drink until you have been weighed, otherwise you will automatically be reported for exclusion. If you have misjudged your kart weight, and are found to be under the class weight, you should get a second chance to weigh. Try the kart and yourself on a different orientation on the scales, and maybe ask politely for the check weights to be tried. Otherwise accept the inevitable, sign the forms, and visit the Clerk of the Course. There are no points on your licence for technical offences.

Meeting with the Clerk of the Course

If you are called up to see the Clerk of the Course, it is either because you have been reported by a marshal or observer for poor driving standards, or you have been sinned against and they want to hear your side of the story before deciding on any penalty. If, however, you suspect that you are the sinner, then it might be a good idea to find a witness who is willing to give a version of the incident favourable to yourself; this could be another following competitor, or an onlooker.

If the hearing is about something you were not aware of, for example being accused of passing on a yellow flag, then depending on the evidence against you it is usually good to apologise in the hope of a minimum penalty.

If you are accused of causing an incident, then either admit it and apologise, or if you think you are being wronged, ask if your witness can come in to the hearing. Unless you are very sure of your grounds of innocence, then it is not normally worth the expense of appealing the decision to the stewards of the meeting. You will be given thirty minutes from the decision to make an appeal, accompanied by the correct fee. Always remember that if under eighteen, a driver must be accompanied by the person who counter-signed their entry.

The Clerk of the Course has a range of sanctions available, from a reprimand, a monetary fine, a time or place penalty, to exclusion from the race or even exclusion from the whole meeting. Usually a driving penalty will be accompanied by a number of penalty points applied to the competition licence, and once twelve points have been accrued in a twelve-month penalty, the driver's licence will automatically be withdrawn for a period of time. The MSA steward can access the MSA licence details to find out how many points are already on a licence, and if necessary confiscate it on the day. Technical offences in kart racing do not usually have penalty points applied.

Remaining Heats and Last Chance Races

Between the heats check over and prepare your kart for the next race: replenish the fuel, make any adjustments to the chassis, engine or tyre pressures, and be on time at the dummy grid; also, always check the result of the preceding race as you only get thirty minutes to make a complaint. Once the heats are over there may be a short lunch break whilst the organizers work out the grids for

A warning flag is given to the driver whose number is shown.

the finals. If there is a large entry in your class, be aware there could be a B or even a C final, and you need to be ready in case you are in one of those.

The names of those involved will normally be posted on the notice board, in grid order, but could just be shouted over the tannoy. If you are in one of these last chance races do your utmost to get into the top four,

because normally these are elevated to the back of the next final. If you don't, that will be the end of your day's racing, your chances of further points, and maybe even trophies – but maybe it won't, either, because most clubs give a novice trophy, and if you are the best novice, even if not in the A final, it is worth asking, or waiting for the prize-giving.

Make sure you go to the prize-giving to applaud the trophy winners.

The A Final

The A final will normally be longer than the heats, so be sure to put in extra fuel. You may want to drop the tyre pressures slightly, as they will heat up more in the longer race. Once you become accustomed to setting up the kart, you can choose for optimum speed at the start, or at the end of the race. If you set up the kart to 'come on' quickly, if you are at the front of the grid you may be able to get away from the rest of the pack, but at risk of being caught up later and having to strongly defend your position. You might think doing this is a good idea, too, if you are near the back and think fast progression in the early stages is likely to pay off. However, it is usually better to have the kart come on strongly in the later stages of the race, so you can attack as other drivers start to fade.

After the Race

Your kart or engine may be selected for a full eligibility check, when parts may be stripped for inspection and checking. You or your mechanic must do any disman-tling, then the scrutineer will ask for certain parts and will measure them and check them against the regu-lations.

When you come in and are finished with scruti-neering, you might find a race reporter looking for a quote. Start with a brief description of your race, why you enjoyed it or otherwise, and remember to thank your mechanic, team and supporters. Do say something positive – if you are known for giving good quotes they will come back to you again. Now is the time to have a coffee or energy stimulant drink, to get through the prize-giving and packing-up process.

If you left your licence with the organizers for a signature, go and collect it. It might not be released until thirty minutes after the end of your last race, when the time to protest has run out. Remember to update your notebook with your settings for the final, and your finishing position, and remember to collect any beacon you had out for your data logger. Look for a

Your engine may be dismantled to check for eligibility.

race result sheet to take home, but if you can only find the noticeboard copy, write down your fastest time and the overall fastest for comparison. If you can, thank the club officials and organizers – and remember to drive safely on the way home.

Marshalling

You will have seen the number of officials and marshals needed to organize a race meeting, so why not volunteer to be a marshal for a day? It can be a great way to see the racing close up, and to learn about other aspects of the sport.

Championships

CHAPTER 7

Most drivers want to compare themselves with others, either in a single race weekend or over a series of races that are amalgamated into a championship. Club championships are usually termed non commercial, and although there might be vouchers or goods as end-of-year prizes, most likely there will be just trophies and honour at stake. As drivers progress, however, many will wish to move on to national and even international championships, budget permitting. Most of these competitions will be held over a series, but some are staged over just a single weekend. Prestigious titles are at stake, for instance British, European and World Champion. Kart racing is on a par with Formula 1 and rally driving in having FIA-recognized world championship titles.

Even if a driver is not the winner of the title, the thrill and goal is to see how far up the championship points

A typically packed championship paddock.

table he can get, and to better it the following year. Champions are revered, and looked up to as the pace setters. Very often a champion will be able to use the number '1', or some other recognized symbol as his or her competition number. In nationally recognized MSA British or ABKC national championships, the top nine, ten or fifteen are also permitted to use their positions as their competition numbers for the following year, and no one else should use these numbers. These 'seeded' or 'cherished' numbers give the drivers a status above the others.

CLUB CHAMPIONSHIPS

In MSA authorized racing, everyone starts with a club level race, and in most cases joining the club automatically enters the driver into their club championship. Sometimes novice drivers may not be permitted in the championship, and some clubs have more than one championship per annum, for instance a winter and summer series. Always check the championship regulations, which will have been approved by the MSA, and will be available from the club, perhaps by having it printed in their race day programme, or on their website. In any case it must be made available to the entrants.

Sometimes in a series all the rounds count, in which case it is most important to finish each race, and obviously in as good a position as possible. But very often a certain number of rounds can be 'dropped': this means that the worst scores on a set number of rounds, detailed in the championship regulations, are discarded, and the points for the remaining rounds totalled up to give the final championship positions. Often club championships will allow two or three rounds to be dropped. This gives drivers who may also be competing in national championships that clash on dates, an equal chance in their club series. It also means that a very successful driver may not need to compete in the last round or two, as it is possible they cannot be beaten, no matter what position their rivals attain. However, sometimes the best of the discarded round points are used as a tie decider.

Points Scoring

It cannot be emphasized enough that drivers should read and understand the championship regulations thoroughly,

as there will be nuances that may be exploited to best advantage. In some championship the heats may count for points, in others just the finals. Often the points will be biased towards the winner of each race, so if, for instance, the winner gets forty points, the second might get thirty-five, third thirty-two, fourth thirty, and the remainder one point less per position. It's also important to find out what points are given to non finishers, non starters or excluded drivers, in case that situation occurs. Sometimes penalty points are deducted if a driver is excluded or receives penalty points on their licence, or the round in question must be counted as one of the scores, and not dropped. In fact the default MSA regulations state that if a driver is totally excluded from a race meeting, which usually occurs with a serious technical offence, then the round must be counted and a number of penalty points applied. Luckily, however, most championship series recognize that this is an excessive penalty and waive it in the individual regulations.

The nuances of the regulations may influence how much the driver contests a penalty: in some cases it means he just has to drop that round, in others it may mean his chances of achieving a good championship position have been completely ruined.

Checking the Points

The championship points tables are usually published on the club's web site or noticeboard, and you should check them carefully for accuracy after each round. If it is thought that a mistake has been made, in the first instance the driver should contact the competition secretary. If that still does not result in a correction, drivers or entrants can always make an appeal to the championship stewards, who will be listed in the regulations. Nearly all suspected errors turn out to be a misreading of the regulations, and if a genuine mistake has been made the competition secretary will usually correct it at the next round. Sometimes the computer program that does the lap scoring includes a championship points calculator add on, or perhaps the competition secretary or championship co-ordinator will use a spreadsheet to work out the points and positions.

As the championship comes to the last few rounds, start doing your own calculations to find out the best and worst case final positions. Deduct the worst scores for the number of possible dropped rounds, and add back the maximum possible scores for your rivals and yourself, to see if you can be beaten to a position.

Moving On

Many drivers will be content to compete at their local club, but those with higher aspirations and a big enough budget may wish to move on to a national or international series.

NATIONAL CHAMPIONSHIPS

There is only one national championship per class which is authorized to issue the seeded numbers. At the time of writing the Super One Series holds the MSA British Championship for juniors and seniors, and the Association of British Kart Club (ABKC) National Championships for Rotax, TKM and Honda Cadet classes. Formula Kart Stars (FKS) holds the contract for the MSA British Cadet Kart Championship and non-national series for Rotax junior classes. The Super One also offers a Comer Cadet series. Note that the contracts end in 2012, and in 2013 there may be a new engine for the Cadet classes, which would become the official national or British series. Easykart also hold a championship series. These are all held at specific race meetings, exclusive to these individual championships.

Other organizations may offer multi-round, multi-venue championships or challenges that are usually guested at club meetings. Sometimes separate races will be held for these guest classes at the club meetings, or sometimes the guest championship contenders will fit into the club's normal race programme, and have their points allocated on the places achieved.

For long circuit, the Superkart club holds the MSA Long-Circuit Kart Championship in the 250cc class, and offers support races in 125cc and 210 national classes.

Choosing a Championship

The competitor will have to decide whether to plunge into one of the main national championships or try one of the lesser series first; this will also be decided by his ability and budget. To compete in the national championships the competitor must hold a National A licence, so must have received signatures from the MSA steward in a minimum of eleven races at three venues. There may be further pre-qualification required: for instance the British Cadet championship may have a minimum age, or the competitor may have to have attained a sufficient level in a club championship or in a qualifying race or races to prove they are sufficiently competent. The standard at the front of the national championships is very high, as many of the same competitors race and do well in the international series, so a competitor new to the series must expect a further period of learning and improving their own abilities. However, there is nothing like pitching oneself against the best in the country to improve skills.

On the other hand, starting with one of the lesser status multi-round series gives drivers a chance to try their skills at different tracks against more experienced competitors.

Multi-round, Multi-venue Championships

Some of the karting associations offer multi-round, multi-venue championships that visit different club meetings, for example the Northern Karting Federation (NKF). To enter, competitors complete a registration form and pay a registration fee, which for this type of series is usually quite modest. Then the entry fee is paid to each club visited, sometimes with a small surcharge added on, which goes to the championship organizers to help pay for series officials and other costs such as trophies or prizes.

The costs of undertaking such challenges will be much less than the official national championships, because such additional costs as controlled issue tyres and fuel are unlikely. Even some of the national championships are guested at club meetings because there are not enough competitors in the class to make up a stand-alone series. For instance, this applies to the gearbox classes: the KZ2 UK (125cc) and 250 National have an ABKC national championship called the Super 4, whilst the 210 National classes have a Challenge series.

National and British Championship Series

Generally competitors have to register for the series by the end of January each year, although if the class is not full up, then registrations can sometimes be made later. Often guest drivers are permitted, if they want to try it out, or race at their local club against the best. As well as the registration fee, competitors may have to pay for some of the individual round entry fees in advance; this is so that the clubs at the tail end of the year do not suffer from a drop in income if some competitors decide to withdraw.

Typically these prestige championships have higher costs and much more stringent rules and timetables. Tyres have to be paid for in advance, sometimes both wets and slicks, and they will be issued after drawing lots. To avoid cheating by adding any tyre-softening substances, the tyres will usually be kept in *parc fermé* and only issued to the competitor just before each race.

When the race is over the competitor will hand back his tyres before leaving the controlled area, the *parc fermé* as it is called. There will be specific times in the programme to have the tyres issued and marked for that competitor, and for the competitor or his mechanic to fit the tyres on to

A podium at a Super One British Championship meeting.

Tyres are kept in parc fermé *and issued to competitors before each race at major championships.*

the rims. No substances will be allowed into the area – tyre soap and compressed air to aid fitting will be on hand. If it is permitted for tyres to be used for more than one round they are sometimes placed in a sealed bag so the competitor can bring them to the next round. If the seal is broken, they will have to purchase new tyres.

Control fuel is another expense associated with major championships. To avoid cheating, a specific fuel is specified, containing a marker which is easily recognized by the equipment used for checking. To make it easier to check that the fuel has not been modified, sometimes only a specific oil can be used for the two-stroke classes. Again the fuel has to be ordered and paid for in advance, and a specific time will be given in the programme for its issue at the track. The very major international championships will also keep the fuel tanks from each kart in *parc fermé* between races.

There may be other compulsory items to purchase or hire, for instance clutch logging equipment or video cameras. Clutch loggers are fitted to karts to detect excessive slip on the clutch, which may indicate an attempt to cheat through modifying or adding oil or grease and gain an advantage out of slow corners. Miniature video cameras are used for judicial purposes, to see who might be at fault in an incident.

At any high level championship it is very important to study the timetable and be sure to attend everything relevant at the correct time without fail. Not attending something could have serious consequences, ranging from a fine to exclusion; similarly making a mistake on the scrutineering card with an engine, chassis or seal number could result in exclusion. So check and double check; read the regulations carefully, and remember how much time is given for each task before the grid closes for a race.

Competitors must use the designated control fuel at major meetings.

Video cameras mounted on the kart are often used for judicial purposes as well as for television coverage.

Super One Series

The Super One Series is the longest running and largest national championship in the UK, having started in 1983. It offers, or has in the past, offered championships for the international KF classes, the Rotax classes and the TKM classes for both juniors and seniors; it also has championships for the Cadet classes. In recent years the series has been televised.

The Super One Series started as one series, then as the number of classes expanded it split into separate junior and senior classes. As the Rotax classes became the predominant choice for both juniors and seniors these sustained a series of their own, with separate series for TKM two- and four-stroke, and another series for Cadets and the international classes. More recently the series contracted to two parallel seven-round series for Rotax and Honda Cadet, and the other for the international classes, Cadets, Super Cadets and TKM two-stroke.

There is a large prize fund, split between cash and goods or vouchers. Drivers who do well in the Super One Series also compete very successfully on the international stage, proving that the British system is one of the best in the world. This is generally attributed to the club racing system of having heats where drivers start from a front, middle or back position, which forces them to learn how to overtake. Then when they come to the major championships they learn the art of timed qualifying to set their initial grid positions. Overtaking becomes harder as the drivers have already been graded according to their speed. Indy 500 winner Daniel Wheldon won the Super One Cadet championship in 1990, and F1 driver Jenson Button a year later.

Formula Kart Stars

The Formula Kart Stars series concentrates on Cadets and juniors and is a stepping stone to the racing car industry. It has been supported by Formula One management, and many of the prizes comprise scholarships into the racing car industry. At the time of writing it holds the contract for the MSA British Cadet Championship, and has support championships for MiniMax and Junior Max. The series started in 1996 as 'Champions of the Future', then was renamed 'Stars of the Future' before its present title.

Most of the current and recently famous British racing drivers have competed in both series, for example Jenson Button, Anthony Davidson, Daniel Wheldon, Lewis Hamilton and Paul Di Resta. F1 driver Hamilton won the MSA British Cadet Championship in 1996, and Di Resta won it the year after. By the time these drivers are aged twenty and looking for a F1 seat, they may have been racing for twelve years already.

The end-of-year prize-giving is a major event: this is the Super One Series with old-boy Formula 1 driver Jenson Button giving out the trophies.

INTERNATIONAL CHAMPIONSHIPS

The pinnacles of international racing are the FIA-CIK European and World Championships, held for the internationally recognized KF classes and for Superkarts. The FIA-CIK also has a world championship for under eighteens, known as the U18. A British driver, Jake Dennis, became the inaugural champion in 2010. Other promoters hold international championships for these classes as well, for instance the WSKI (Winning Series Karting International series), which also attracts manufacturer team support.

Commercially backed classes such as Rotax hold an annual grand final, which is marketed as the Olympics of karting because each participating country in the world holds qualifying rounds to choose the drivers to send to these grand finals. There is also a European international Rotax multi-round series, known as EuroMax. Easykart similarly have an international final, with entrants from the best of the various national series, including the UK.

Although not currently successfully promoted in the UK, other commercial classes such as Rok and X30

hold large annual grand finals. There are a number of prestigious one-off annual events with international status, and several countries hold their national series on an international permit, trying to attract drivers from other regions.

Generally speaking, European drivers who are recognized as professionals have the EU flag on their licence and can usually compete in the national events of other European countries. If an event wants to attract drivers from outside the EU, then the promoters can apply to their local ASN to have the event put on the international calendar. This procedure is known as NEAFP: 'national event authorized for foreign participation'. Foreign drivers are permitted to win trophies on the day, but not to accrue points in a series.

THE LADDER OF SUCCESS

It can therefore be seen that the bottom of the pyramid in kart racing is the club championship, and the top the world championship, and for the commercial classes their grand finals.

Kart racing has an FIA-recognized world championship.

FACT

The Motor Racing Ladder of Success

- Club karting championship

- Multi-venue karting championship

- National karting championship

- International karting championship

- European FIA-CIK karting championship

- World karting championship or commercial equivalent

- Junior car racing formulae, such as Formula Ford, Formula Renault

- Formula 2, Formula 3

- GP3, Renault 3.5

- GP2

- Formula 1

There is also the following ladder:

- Junior or senior saloons or sportscars

- British Touring Car Championship

- World Touring Cars

- DTM (German Touring Cars)

- National sportscars

- International sportscars

It is generally agreed that a successful single-seater driver will have competed in Formula 3, but there are many routes to the top of formula cars, saloon cars or sportscars. Many successful kart drivers become professional racing drivers, earning their living from the sport. A very few will become professional kart racing drivers employed by the manufacturer teams. Others who learn their trade in kart racing will become successful engineers or driving coaches, even team managers. Christian Horner, the successful Formula 1 team manager, started as a club kart racer.

TELEVISION, VIDEO, RADIO AND THE PRINT MEDIA

As a driver rises through the ranks to the premier championships they will increasingly catch the public eye. A successful driver will be asked to comment on their race, speak to video cameras, and generally make themselves available to the press. The press representatives love a driver who is agreeable and amenable, even after some track disaster, and they will keep coming back for good quotes. This can only be good for the driver and his sponsors. Courses and training guides are available for drivers who wish to improve their skills in this area.

When attending a podium presentation the driver should ensure their race suit is worn, and either their own sponsor's cap or the one provided by the organizers. They should look happy and smile for the cameras even if they have just lost a race or championship. No racing driver is a good loser, but they must disguise that in public.

The press and the television interviewer are both looking for the same thing: a short, memorable and informative quote. Do not on any account attack your rivals, but remember to thank your sponsors and backers, which may be noted if there is room, even if it is just your parents backing you.

LOOKING AFTER YOUR BACKERS

If you have been lucky enough to attract backers or sponsors, take care to nurture them at every opportunity. There are many occasions when you can give them something in return for their investment, some at quite low cost, as the following suggestions show:

- A visit to the race track
- A hospitality package at the race track
- The opportunity to mix with like-minded business men and women
- Publicity in local and national media
- Web site and social media updates
- Prizes or goodies to distribute
- Display of the kart at business premises
- Display of the kart at local shows or exhibitions

Always ensure a report goes to all of them on the Monday following a race meeting to update your progress.

Certainly your sponsors will expect their company names on your kart and overalls, and if they are sufficiently exclusive, perhaps a complete body kit in their colours; this could extend to sign-writing on your van or trailer. You need to ensure, either directly or through their own PR department, that regular reports are placed in the local press, and any relevant news items into the national specialist press. Local radio is often much more amenable to carrying sports news than regional television, but keep trying.

Nowadays most of the target audience will be fully conversant with the internet, so full use must be made of web sites, blogs and social media such as Facebook, Twitter and LinkedIn. Short videos could be posted on YouTube. Keep the messages short and factual, but most of all keep the sites up to date, and always mention the date and venue of the next event.

MAKING THE BEST USE OF SUPPORT

If you have been lucky enough to receive an amount of some consequence, then you should have a contract, or at least exchange a letter of understanding about what each party expects from the partnership. The most common help is with product support, when a supplier, shop or trader might offer to supply you with free consumables of some kind, in exchange for you carrying their decals on your kart. Try and get some extra free samples to distribute amongst your fellow drivers: you might persuade them to use the same consumables, which will please your sponsor.

Next in line might be that your sponsor offers to buy some of the equipment, for instance a new kart or engine, or they might agree to pay the entry fees or

Support vehicles as well as the karts may be sign written.

purchase tyres or fuel for the year. Finally they might offer cash help. In these cases be honest and clear about any tax implications for both parties.

Skilled, successful drivers are sometimes loaned a free kart and/ or engine for the season. However, just be sure that the kart is a competitive proposition: there is no use in having free equipment if it isn't able to perform. A race team may offer a free drive for the season, because if they have a successful winning driver on board it attracts paying drivers. So be sure to help these other drivers in the team whenever possible, as their funds are in effect paying for your drive. At the end of the season it is often the case that a modest sum will secure the equipment, even if you decide to sell it on later.

SCHOLARSHIPS

Poverty-stricken drivers need to find any possible route to the top, and scholarships can play a part. Large companies, sometimes race teams, or foundations may support drivers from a young age. They do this to get a pay-back, and almost certainly you will have to sign a long-term contract

signing over a percentage of future earnings to them. Take independent legal advice at this stage. The backers may also have the say in which team you are placed in each year, and set targets for continued support. Your media skills will have to be honed to perfection, and it may be very worthwhile taking a course in the subject.

Towards the end of each season race team managers for the next level up will send spotters to the final rounds of the major championships. They will be after good drivers with sufficient budget for the next step.

The other type of scholarship is the multi-round commercial type, where a prize is on offer to the winner. The many rejected entrants in effect are paying for the one or two successful winners. Again be careful about contracts, and do not sign your future away for little actual reward. However, there have been some very good car racing scholarships of this type, giving impecunious drivers a chance to reach the top.

And finally a scholarship may be offered as a prize in a championship. Make sure that what is being offered is given in writing, because you can be absolutely sure that there will be many add-on costs necessary for a successful season.

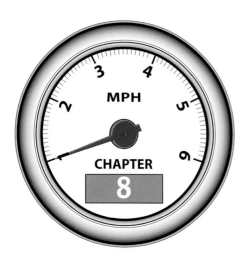

Governance of the Sport

GOVERNANCE OVERVIEW

Newly licensed drivers will come into contact with the MSA (Motor Sports Association) when they apply for their first competition licence. Thereafter they will have more immediate contact with their local club officials and MSA-licensed volunteer officials. Some of those they meet in the course of their kart-racing career may well be on one or more of the MSA specialist committees which propose and amend the regulations. The twenty-four-strong Motor Sports Council (MSC) is actually the body that ratifies any changes to regulations, and also appoints the National Court. Any disputes or appeals which are not held at the actual race meeting will be referred to the National Court for adjudication. Occasionally a driver may meet with the salaried members of the MSA. The MSA can be thought of as the Civil Service, and the MSC as the parliament, but would be more accurately described as the Sporting Commission.

The MSA is the appointed body (the ASN) for the governance of four-wheeled motor sport in the UK, whilst internationally the FIA (Fédération Internationale de l'Automobile) with its subsidiary the CIK (Commission Internationale de Karting) is responsible for kart racing.

FIA/CIK offices at a meeting.

THE MOTOR SPORTS ASSOCIATION

The RAC (Royal Automobile Club) embraced the new sport of kart racing in 1959 and set some initial regulations. In the early years there were up to 100 different manufacturers, and the sport attracted famous racing drivers and many spectators. The RAC rules set minimum age limits, which over the years have been gradually reduced: at the time of writing youngsters can compete in Bambino karts from the age of six, and in Cadets at eight. The RAC also formed a Kart Committee to look after the sport.

In 1975 the RAC formed the Motor Sports Council, and in 1979 the RAC Motor Sports Association was created. When the RAC was sold, the Motor Sports Association became an independent body, a 'not for profit' organization. Its headquarters are at Colnbrook, near Heathrow airport.

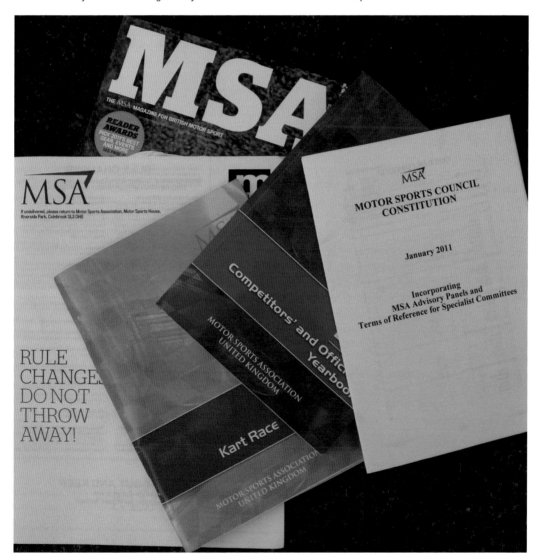

MSA publications.

Committee Structure

Specialist committees for each motor sport discipline review their relevant regulations and advise the MSC when changes are needed. There are also specialist sub-committees and advisory panels responsible for safety, judicial, medical, technical and timekeeping issues, and for volunteer officials. The committees and panels are largely made up of volunteers drawn from competitors, officials, clubs, organizers and administrators. Most often the secretariat for each committee will be from the permanent (approximately thirty-five) members of staff of the MSA. Many clubs belong to a regional association, and are represented through them on the MSA Regional Committee.

Other MSA Activities

The MSA also has a commercial subsidiary named the International Motor Sports Ltd which organizes events such as the British Grand Prix and the International Rally of Great Britain, amongst other things. The MSA puts out tenders and awards contracts for British championships in all the disciplines. It is funded primarily from licence and event permit fees, and promotes motor sport in many ways, including young driver support. Go Motorsport and Let's Go Karting are examples of initiatives designed to involve the public and make them aware of the possibilities of participating in motor sport activities. There are funds available to help clubs and relevant organizations.

The MSA is also empowered to authorize the use of public highways in England and Wales for motor sport, and has an arrangement with the Forestry Commission for the use of its woodland tracks by rally vehicles. Of course the MSA publishes the *Competitors Year Book* (the 'Blue Book') and the *Kart Race Yearbook* (the 'Gold Book'), which contain all the regulations. It has also formulated a child protection policy, which extends to all clubs involved with minors, and it organizes CRB checks for motor sport volunteers. There are training schemes for officials, with regular seminars to keep them updated.

Facts and Figures

Most of the MSA income is derived from the sale of 30,000-plus competition licences, of which almost 5,000 are for kart racing. An important part of the MSA is their responsibility for the insurance of motor sport events. Drivers pay for this through a 'per capita' part of their entry fees. Some 750 clubs are recognized, of which about thirty are active kart clubs.

The National Court

If a dispute from a race meeting is referred to the National Court, they may sit to adjudicate. Appeals can be made against the decision of the stewards of the meeting on the grounds of a gross miscarriage of justice, or if it felt that the penalty is wholly inappropriate. If accepted, then a hearing will be set up. Usually one or more of the members of the National Court will be an experienced lawyer. The appellant is also allowed to have an advocate, and to call witnesses. If the dispute is over an alleged technical eligibility issue, then the stewards at the race meeting will not be deemed competent to make a decision, and will refer the matter to an Eligibility Appeal Panel. Generally this is adjudicated on the written submissions of both parties and there will be no right to an oral hearing.

THE FIA AND CIK

As mentioned above, the FIA is the internationally recognized body for controlling motor sport. Its headquarters are in Paris. The CIK-FIA regulates karting activities around the world, and is one of the sporting commissions of the FIA. The CIK has its headquarters in Geneva. Very often the MSA will be able to appoint representatives to the CIK International Karting Commission and to the CIK Technical Working Group, and thus influence the regulations. The CIK also organizes world and European race championship events, and sets the safety, sporting and technical regulations for the internationally recognized classes.

Also, through a process called homologation, basic components such as the chassis, engine, tyres and bodywork, and ancillary components such as air intake boxes and exhausts, are regulated and approved for a period – this is usually for an initial six years, extendable to nine. The CIK will also award contracts for components such as tyres, fuel and carburettors for their championships.

THE COMMITTEE STRUCTURE

There is a chain of representation for the competitor all the way up from club committee level to the top of the MSA committee structure.

Club Committee

Kart clubs are always on the lookout for new members to join their committees. MSA-affiliated clubs must have an approved constitution, which will allow for annual general meetings where prospective committee members can be nominated and elected. The club committee is responsible for the promotion of its race meetings through the appointment of officials such as the competition and race secretary, the Clerk of the Course, chief and eligibility scrutineers, official timekeepers and so on. It will also draw up its supplementary and championship regulations, which must be approved by the MSA. The intention to apply for a championship permit must be made in the September of the previous year. The MSA publishes a *Motor Club Manual* to assist volunteers in running a club and promoting events, which is available on their website.

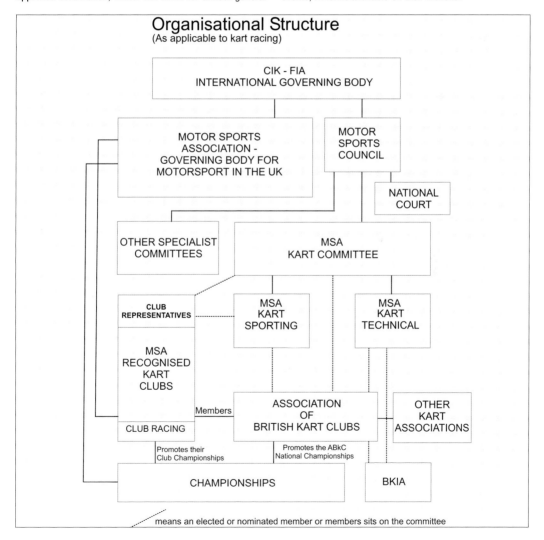

Organisational Structure
(As applicable to kart racing)

- CIK - FIA INTERNATIONAL GOVERNING BODY
- MOTOR SPORTS ASSOCIATION - GOVERNING BODY FOR MOTORSPORT IN THE UK
- MOTOR SPORTS COUNCIL
- NATIONAL COURT
- OTHER SPECIALIST COMMITTEES
- MSA KART COMMITTEE
- CLUB REPRESENTATIVES
- MSA KART SPORTING
- MSA KART TECHNICAL
- MSA RECOGNISED KART CLUBS
- Members
- CLUB RACING
- ASSOCIATION OF BRITISH KART CLUBS
- OTHER KART ASSOCIATIONS
- Promotes their Club Championships
- Promotes the ABkC National Championships
- CHAMPIONSHIPS
- BKIA

.... means an elected or nominated member or members sits on the committee

ABkC meeting.

Regional Kart Associations

There are a number of kart associations, some of them regional and some national, such as the Association of British Kart Clubs (ABkC). Scotland and Northern Ireland have strong regional associations which organize championships in their areas, visiting the various club events in their regions. The ABkC has multiple roles for its thirty or so member clubs. Primarily it was formed in 1990 to act as an interface between kart clubs and the MSA. The MSA offers seats on its main karting committees to ABkC representatives.

Clubs have the opportunity to nominate and elect members to the ABkC steering group – the management committee – every year. The rest of the steering group consists of representatives of the regional associations, the British and major national championship organizers, the trade, and observers from the MSA. Therefore there are experts from every facet of karting available to draw upon when proposing changes in regulations, or discussing the classes that the ABkC promotes. It promotes the sport through various avenues, primarily by publishing an annual guide on how to start karting, along with a DVD, as well as exhibiting at major motor sport shows.

Another role of the ABkC has been to award contracts for a single nominated type of tyre for each of the classes it supports. Prior to the formation of the ABkC it was possible for different clubs to use different tyres for the same class. By ensuring that all its member clubs nominate the same tyre, drivers can move freely from club to club and race using the same equipment.

Finally the ABkC awards the contracts for the major national championships. Every few years it chooses a promoter for the main classes, and ensures that all its member clubs recognize the seeded or cherished numbers that are awarded to the top ten or fifteen drivers in each class. It also chooses clubs to hold the annual ABkC 'O' Plates, the Open Championships.

In the early 1990s, the MSA stopped publishing detailed kart class regulations in its 'Blue Book' so the ABkC took over the role, and published them in its 'Green Book'. More recently, the MSA took back the responsibility of publishing the class regulations in the MSA *Kart Race Yearbook*, known as the 'Gold Book'.

MSA Committees

The MSA's Kart Committee is made up of two delegates appointed from each of six regions – the Midlands, the South West and South Wales, the South East and East Anglia, Northern England and North Wales, Scotland and Northern Ireland – plus a representative of the ABkC and of the MSA. It is supported by sub-committees of Kart Sporting and Kart Technical. These sub-committees will advise the Kart Committee on regulation changes in sporting and technical matters respectively, and their chairpersons also sit on the Kart Committee. All changes are promulgated on the MSA website before being referred to council for ratification. During this consultation period, comments are welcomed, and the committee will take these into account and possibly revise the proposal for final ratification.

Lap scoring is only one of many volunteer official posts needed at race meetings.

Competitors can have input through their club committee, direct to the ABKC secretary for discussion at the next steering group meeting, or to the MSA executives for tabling at meetings of the relevant MSA committees.

CLUB ORGANIZATION

As mentioned above, clubs are always keen for volunteers, whether for marshals, officials or joining the committee. Kart clubs are in effect small businesses, some turning over several hundred thousand pounds per annum. The committee needs a chairman, secretary, competition secretary, treasurer, chief marshal and PR person at a minimum. Some clubs own their race circuit, others will rent a circuit for their race meetings. Either the club or the circuit owner will offer practice days, which will be covered by their own insurance, whilst insurance during MSA-permitted race days is covered by the MSA through a levy on the entry fee. Clubs also need to supply two stewards, to join the MSA steward for any adjudication.

Every club will have a web site, which is the first point of reference for information.

The MSA's kart committee meeting at Colnbrook.

Data-Logging

DATA-LOGGING ESSENTIALS

Data-logging has become an essential part of almost all motor-racing activities these days, and karting is no exception. Analysing and using the data to make changes to the kart or engine can take out much of the guesswork and speed up the convergence to the optimum settings if used intelligently. If a comparison can be made with the data from another faster driver on the same equipment, that is even better. Some teams will even employ a dedicated data analysis engineer.

But data-logging should not be the sole method used. The coach or mechanic should also be using a stopwatch and taking the split times of the rival drivers whose data will not be accessible, as well as of his own driver for direct comparisons. The coach must also ask the driver for their 'feel' of the kart at each corner.

A record must always be kept of each change to the kart, and when it was changed, so that it can be related directly to the stored data when it is reviewed later. Accurate and effective file management is therefore also very important.

The dashboard display can often be set to show an alarm when a parameter goes beyond the normal range, for instance water temperature. It can often also be set to show when to change gear, by illuminating a series of lights.

The dashboard display can provide the driver with a great deal of relevant information.

On-board video is being used more and more to augment the data from the sensors on the kart – but remember that in races, permission to carry a video camera must be obtained in writing. Young drivers can probably relate faster to the video picture and feedback from their coach, than to analysing complex data traces.

It is very important to keep all cables and connectors in good condition, and all cable runs tidy and safe from chafing. Undue stress on a connector will lead to failure. Keeping on top of these matters will help to ensure the reliability of these devices.

SIMPLE REV-COUNTERS AND LAP-TIMERS

The simplest form of data-logging is a rev-counter with a peak rpm memory mounted on the steering wheel. This is most useful in direct-drive karts without gears, as the memory will show the maximum rpm that the engine attains on a lap. Beware that wheelspin, maybe caused by going wide over a kerb on to grass, can give a false result.

The maximum rpm figure is used to help make a choice for the gearing of the kart, so if the rpm is below the optimum maximum recommended by the engine manufacturer, a sprocket with more teeth can be fitted on the rear axle. This is known as 'adding teeth'. Conversely, if the engine is over-revving, then fewer teeth are needed on the rear sprocket. The maximum rpm on such a simple device is of little use in a geared kart, as inevitably the maximum revs will be seen in the lower gears, and not in top gear where the overall gearing choice is required.

The rev-counter picks up the ignition spark with an insulated wire lead wrapped round the ignition HT lead, or perhaps just clipped to it over a few centimetres. There will be settings on the instrument for two- or four-stroke engines, and for the number of cylinders, so the correct rpm is displayed.

The next level is for the rev-counter to have a continuous recording memory such that a trace of the engine revs over a whole lap can be replayed. Some rev-counters can replay this on their own screen or dial, but ideally the memory would be downloaded on to a laptop. The trace is made more readable if the start and finish of the lap is also shown.

The finish line will have a loop for transponder timing and a magnetic strip for on-board lap timers.

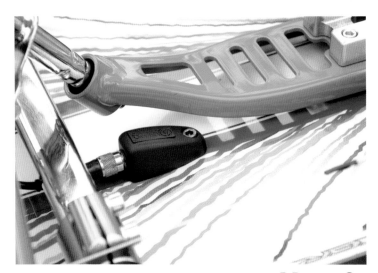

A small pick-up on the floor-tray of the kart detects the buried magnetic strips on the track.

Racing circuits have one or more magnetic strips embedded in the tarmac, always with one at the finish line next to the loop used by the transponders and lap-timing equipment. Most of the simpler types of combined rev-counter and lap-timer employ a sensor on the kart's floor-tray to signal when they cross a magnetic strip. The number of strips at the track is input to the instrument beforehand, and if there is more than one, then sector times can be read. The lap-timer will have a memory so that the lap times can be read back later, or maybe downloaded to a laptop. Usually each time the kart crosses the finish line, the lap-timer can be set to show the previous lap time so that the driver can read it at the next opportunity, usually the next straight when the workload is less.

Some will show a delta, meaning the plus or minus time to the fastest lap achieved in the session. Be aware that the lap-timer may pick up the first strip out of the pits and carry on lap-timing at that point, rather than the official time at the finish line.

Now that the lap times and lap start or finish point are known, a download of the rpm trace for each lap can be seen, and the rpm at each corner apex easily identified.

The next step is for the data-logger to show a circuit map on the laptop screen, combined with a wheel-speed sensor, so the distance travelled can be combined with the other data and compared with subsequent laps or sessions.

MORE COMPLEX DATA-LOGGING

Data-loggers can have a multitude of sensors attached, but the more sensors there are, the more skill is required to interpret and make use of the data. Some data-loggers require a beacon to be placed at the side of the track, which is picked up on each lap by the kart equipment. This is an alternative to the type that uses a sensor to pick up a magnetic strip embedded in the track, and of course if a beacon can be used it is independent of any track facilities. It is best to place the beacon at the finish line, so the lap times are read at the same point as the official timing. Permission should be sought to enter the track and place the beacon.

The more complex data-loggers might have a separate unit for the collection and processing of all the sensor inputs, with a display head mounted on the steering wheel. The manufacturer will offer computer software used to download and display the telemetry. Often the computer applications are freely available on websites so the latest version can easily be downloaded.

Sensors

As already mentioned, the rpm is picked up by a wire on to the spark plug HT ignition lead. The beacon will either be a pick-up mounted low down, usually on the floor-tray, to detect magnetic strips, while more sophisticated

Possible Sensors

- RPM
- Beacon or magnetic strip sensor input for lap-times
- Wheel-speed sensor(s)
- X-Y accelerometers measuring at minimum lateral G
- Engine coolant temperature
- Throttle pedal sensor
- Brake pedal sensor
- Steering angle
- Exhaust or cylinder head temperature
- Tyre temperature
- GPS

attached to the front wheel rim or the rear axle. It is best to tape the magnet on.

Alternatively they can detect a gap in, for instance, a brake disc, and can be set so the number of gaps is taken into account when calculating speed. In all cases the circumference of the tyre must be input to the logger, so speed and distance can be calculated. When tyres or tyre pressure are changed, always recheck the circumference. Also use the circumference when the tyre is hot, and remeasure it occasionally as the tyres wear. Other errors creep in because the tyres will 'grow' in size as the kart goes faster. This can be a problem in long-circuit superkarts.

Using the rear axle can give errors due to wheel spin on accelerating, and also if the wheels are locked up on braking. Using a front wheel can also give errors if they are braked and lock up, but that is less usual. The outer front wheel will describe a longer distance round a corner than the inner rear wheel, which can also lead to small errors. Very sophisticated loggers may have a sensor on both front wheels and use the average, or have an additional sensor on the rear axle for comparison. Use the outer front wheel as a preference.

A special kind of logger is used by organizers to detect illegal clutch slip. This will compare rear axle

loggers will use a beacon, which means the system is independent of any track facilities. If another kart is passing between the sensor on the kart and the beacon, a lap time might be missed, but this is rare. Wheel speed sensors can either be fitted to the front wheel or the rear axle. They usually detect the rotation of a small magnet

A front wheel speed sensor.

speed with rpm, and if there is a discrepancy in the rate of change, the clutch might be slipping more than is allowed.

The accelerometer should be mounted on the floor-tray just in front of the seat so it is as central as possible; sometimes, however, it is incorporated into the processor unit. Very often the engine-coolant thermo sensor will be mounted in a T-piece a few centimetres from the actual cylinder head, so it will always read a little less than the actual water temperature in the cylinder head. Pedal sensors are linear potentiometers linked to the pedal by a short cable; they usually incorporate a spring so the sensor is not forced past its limit. They need to be zeroed before use within the set-up of the processor. The steering-wheel angle is usually measured by mounting a 360-degree sensor linked by a rubber band to the steering column. Again it needs to be zeroed with the steering in the straight-ahead position.

Exhaust temperature is measured with a probe in the exhaust pipe, close to or incorporated into the outlet manifold. Cylinder head temperature is measured with a thermocouple fitted under the spark plug, either with the usual washer or to replace the washer.

Be aware that many class regulations limit the number and type of sensors permitted. It may be they can be used during practice sessions but not during racing. Once the basic sensors of lap-timing, rpm, wheel speed and hence distance can be determined, the engine gearing can be closely studied. The effect of changes should be clear – for instance, is it better to have a bigger rear sprocket to help acceleration out of slow corners at the expense of over-revving on the longest straight?

A sensor for the throttle pedal position.

A temperature gauge thermocouple sensor.

Tyre Temperature

Only the most sophisticated systems and highly skilled professional teams will measure tyre temperature on the move. Infra-red pick-ups can be mounted on a short bar in front of the tyre, with pick-ups close to the two outer edges and the centre of the tyre, and these can glean valuable information about tyre performance and the optimization of tyre use.

OTHER SYSTEMS

GPS

Systems that can calculate the exact position of a kart on the surface of the earth are becoming sufficiently accurate to be able to trace the path of a kart round the circuit. However, they need to detect enough satellites and calculate the position sufficiently quickly to be accurate. The sensor needs to be mounted at the top of the kart where it has a clear view of the maximum number of satellites. The trace can often then be superimposed on the Google Earth map of the circuit. Apps for smartphones are available which can do the same, but probably not with the same accuracy.

Video Camera

A video camera can be linked into some data-loggers, or a separate video camera could be used and displayed at the same time as the data analysis. The images can give valuable information to the coach – they might display the steering wheel movement, and the pedal or feet movements. The video might also be used to record an overtaking move.

Simulators

Video games or more sophisticated race simulators can be useful if the circuit to be visited is included or can be downloaded. Simulators such as r-factor are not expensive, and many different types of kart and kart circuit are available on the web. They can be used for gaining circuit knowledge, and even to see the effects of changing the parameters set up on the kart.

Kart simulators are becoming more common, often based on computer games.

Using the Data

When the telemetry data is downloaded to a laptop the circuit map can be calculated. The software calculates the turns and straights by using the accelerometer and distance travelled, or if a GPS sensor is employed, but calculation is from the satellite data. Very often the map will not be accurate initially and will need adjusting to make it look like the real thing. Sometimes circuit maps already optimized will be available for download and use.

The data from the sensors can then be displayed on a graph against either time or distance. The better the data-logger, the more times it will have sampled the data in the period of a second. Data can be 'noisy' and initially unusable, so it needs to be electronically filtered so that it appears smoothed out on the trace. If filtered too much then information on spikes or troughs can be lost.

If the logger is using the magnetic strips on the track to determine split times, these will be absolutely fixed every lap. The disadvantage is that there may not be enough to make sensible interpretations. Therefore most software will allow the user to set so-called 'soft' split times, based on the distance travelled from a set point, usually the beacon. These are not quite as accurate, because the driver might take slightly different lines and therefore travel slightly different distances, but it is the only way to compare faster and slower laps, or between different drivers.

If there is access to more than one driver's data the most common first comparisons are between wheel speeds at the braking point, and the minimum speed round the corner. Of course these parameters can be compared on different laps or sessions for the same driver.

Some teams employ dedicated data engineers to analyse the downloads from the karts to help the competitor go faster.

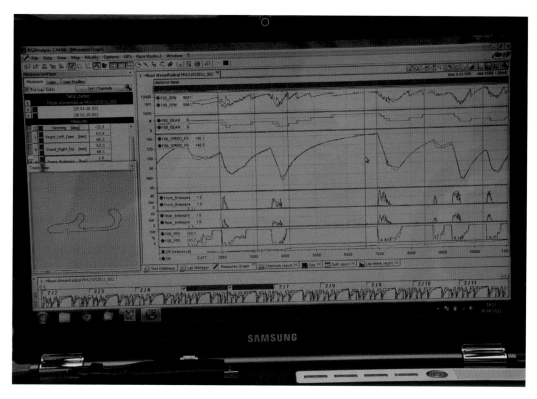

A typical series of traces on a computer screen.

Engine Data

Some computer software can even be used to give a measure of the kart's engine power and torque. In effect, the on-track performance can be used to calculate a torque curve as if the engine were on a dynamometer. Once the optimum power curve is found for a circuit, giving the best times, the kart can then be tuned into finding the same curve at a different track, and should then give the optimum or near-optimum times once again.

159

Engine Care and Rebuilding

CHOOSING A REBUILDING COMPANY

If the engine is sealed, like the Rotax varieties, then all rebuilds will have to be undertaken by an authorized sealer. Even so, there are regular routine maintenance tasks that must take place between these major rebuilds, which will be dealt with later in the chapter. Otherwise the choice is between learning how to maintain and rebuild an engine, or choosing an engine tuner to do the rebuilds. Because of the stresses involved, and the high state of tune, racing engines must be rebuilt at more frequent intervals than regular car or motor-cycle engines. Generally the higher the state of tune, and the higher the rpm used, the more frequently the engine will need rebuilding.

Therefore it is important to keep a running record of the use of the engine, so that the maintenance intervals are not exceeded. There are small devices available that link to the HT ignition lead, and monitor the engine use in hours and minutes. Usually the interval is measured in hours, but sometimes it can be measured in the number of litres of fuel consumed.

So what factors should be taken into account when choosing a rebuilding company? If the engine is sealed then the company must be an authorized agent. These agents are carefully chosen by the engine importer, they will be inspected to ensure they have all the necessary tools, equipment and expertise, and will usually work to an agreed price schedule.

Next to consider is reputation. This can be assessed by seeing whose engines are consistent winners, or by word of mouth from other competitors.

Cost should also be considered. The top tuners may command a higher price, but for beginners a lesser known company may do a perfectly good enough job. Also the locality of the tuner might be worth taking into consideration, so that the engine can be delivered and collected without incurring expensive shipping costs.

Some engine rebuilding companies might be quite happy for the customer to watch while the rebuild is taking place, which could be a useful learning experience. It used to be traditional for an engine rebuilding company to send back in a bag the components that had been replaced, just to prove the work had been done.

If the rebuilding company has access to a dynamometer then the engine can be run in without needing track time, and a power curve generated. Once a power and torque curve has been generated for the engine and compared with the normal curves for the type of engine, advice can be given on whether to vary the gearing up or down a tooth on the rear sprocket compared with the norm for the track in question. This can be assessed on whether the engine is giving its maximum power at slightly higher or lower rpm than normal. If the variance is more than it should be, then something must be amiss, and the rebuilding company should be prepared to find and rectify the problem.

Finally find out whether the engine rebuilder attends the race meetings that are entered, because if they do, then help can be on hand if any problems are encountered or advice needed. If not, see whether they offer a mobile number for weekend use. Build up a rapport with the chosen agent: they want your return custom, and you want good advice when you need it.

ROUTINE ENGINE CARE AND MAINTENANCE

Even if not all the work is done at home, there are routine maintenance tasks which must be done in most engines. First, remove the engine from the kart and seal up all the orifices with plugs of paper wipe towels or rags, or make custom plastic blanking covers fitted with a gasket. Then thoroughly clean the engine with a good de-greaser, using a brush to reach the nooks and crannies, before washing or hosing off.

Once the engine is immaculately clean, disassembly can commence. The correct pullers and tools for certain tasks will have to be purchased, usually from the engine supplier or good kart shops. For some engines a piston stop is needed, to lock the engine whilst the fixing nuts are loosened or tightened. Purchase or download the instruction manual for the engine type. For instance, the manuals for the Rotax engines and the TKM engines are available on-line from the importers or manufacturers; they are full of essential and useful information.

Even if there is no manual available, there will almost certainly be a homologation fiche. In most classes the engines (and sometimes the chassis also) have to be registered, or homologated, with the governing body: this means the engine is eligible in a particular class for a set time, maybe six or nine years. Every few years homologations are offered out for new equipment meeting the regulations, and new engines or chassis are homologated for a new period of time. A special document, or fiche, is drawn

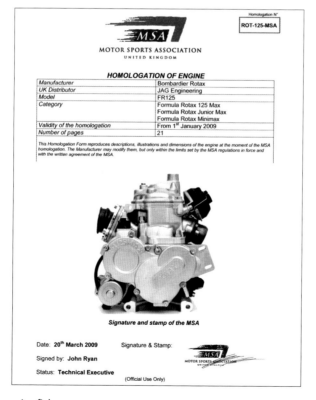

The cover of the Rotax engine fiche.

up with exploded diagrams showing measurements and tolerances of the critical components. So the fiche is a useful source of information. They are available from the engine manufacturer or importer, or if registered with the MSA, will probably be available on the MSA website.

The regulations for some of the smaller classes, and the technical regulations for the Honda GX160 engine, are available on the ABKC website. The regulations for the mainstream classes are contained in the MSA *Kart Race Yearbook*, the 'Gold Book'.

The clutch can be maintained by the user even on sealed engines.

In some engines the water pump is integral, like this one, otherwise it is belt driven from the rear axle.

The oil in the Rotax balance gears needs regular checking and replacement.

The following section describes routine maintenance tasks that can be carried out by the kart owner himself.

Battery: Keep charged, using the correct trickle charger.

Air filter: Clean regularly, and inspect, dry and clean after any wet races or practice sessions. Soap and water is often all that is required, or brake cleaner. Wear protective gloves, and squeeze out and dry.

Sump oil replacement: Replace frequently in four-stroke engines such as the Honda GX-160 – as often as every meeting.

Pull start cord: Inspect and replace – it often breaks just when it is needed to get the kart out for a race, for example for the Comer W60.

Balance gear oil: Replace frequently in engines such as the Rotax 125cc – say, every five hours. Use the correct quantity and type of oil.

Gearbox oil: For gearbox (shifter) engines, replace peri-odically and inspect the used oil for metal particles. If the oil is drained into a container through a clean white cloth, any metal particles will show up on the surface of the cloth. The drain plug will usually have a magnetic element to attract the metal swarf from the wear on the gears, but if this is excessive, have the engine stripped and inspected.

Clutch assembly: Replace when worn; special tools are usually required to loosen and pull off the shaft. In some cases individual parts may be replaced. A large socket is often needed to remove the fixing nut, and it should be tightened to the specification in the manual, and usually fitted with loctite.

Sprocket: Replace when worn.

Ignition: Either to adjust timing for optimum lap times, or to replace if it has failed. It requires a special puller tool.

Crankcase seals: Their life should last between full rebuilds, but if not they can sometimes be hooked out or pressurized out by sealing all orifices and injecting compressed air through the spark plug hole. They are behind the clutch and ignition parts.

Power valve maintenance: The power valve on engine types such as the senior Rotax Max must be kept scrupulously clean and correctly adjusted. Use a material such as Scotchbrite with carb or brake cleaner, but not emery cloth because the surface must be left as original. Ensure it is fitted centrally, and slides in and out easily; if not, keep trying until it is completely free to slide. There is a small range of measurement on the Rotax 125 part, from top to bottom, of 73–75mm.

Decoke (de-carbonize) the cylinder head and piston: If there is an excessive build-up of carbon in the cylinder head and the top of the piston it can be carefully removed – though if the engine is sealed, including the cylinder head, this will not be possible. Build-up might occur if the engine is run with too rich a mixture for too long. In some cases it is not permitted to remove metal or change the surfaces inside the engine, so do not use an abrasive material. A good engine builder will allow a tolerance for the expected amount of carbon build-up.

Reed petals: Inspect the condition of the reed petals in the inlet tract. In a reed valve engine, the petals control the fuel and air mixture intake to the engine, and if they are chipped at the edges or breaking up, then they must be replaced. Note that over-choking engines can be a common reason for damaging the reed petals.

Ignition and electrics: Ensure that all electrical connectors are clean and making good contact; also that the earth wire from the coil to the engine is in good condition – replace if in doubt. Often a second earth cable is used in case the first one breaks during a race.

Exhaust: The exhaust will need decoking, or decarbonising, every so often. There are several ways to remove the carbon, but one method is to soften it by soaking the component for three days in a proprietary brick cleaner. Thereafter it can be washed or pressure hosed off. Afterwards use a water-repellent lubricating spray to prevent rust. The wadding in silencers needs replacing every so often, when the old stuff becomes burnt and brittle.

Starter motor: Occasionally check and replace the brushes. If the commutator has worn out, the motor will need to be replaced. Ensure the fixing bolts are kept tight.

The reed petals are replaceable items.

MAJOR ENGINE REBUILD

At set intervals the complete engine must be stripped down and certain components replaced. Either keep a record of the total time of use of the engine, or attach one of the small digital engine life monitors available.

An engine may run typically for thirty-five minutes at a club meeting, but perhaps twice as long on a practice day. It may be that on some engines, pistons or piston rings may be replaced at half these full rebuild intervals, in which case the whole engine does not need to be dismantled.

On smaller engines such as the Cadet or TKM two-strokes, if a chain is thrown or breaks it may twist the crankshaft, necessitating an early strip-down and rebuild. The need for this can generally be checked if the spark plug is removed, and the engine rotated whilst watching the other end of the crankshaft. If any wobble can be detected by eye (which can discern a $\frac{3}{1000}$in variation), then the engine should be set aside until it can be stripped down.

Stripping Down and Reassembly

After the engine has been thoroughly cleaned, remove all the outer components such as the starter, clutch, sprocket, reed valve assemblies, power valve, ignition and timing parts

An engine completely stripped down.

using the correct tools and pullers. Remove the balance gears, then the cylinder head and cylinder itself, exposing the piston. Press cloths or paper into the crankcase below the piston to catch any falling parts.

Prise out the gudgeon pin circlip to allow the gudgeon pin which holds the piston on to the con-rod, using a very small screwdriver or scribe. If the piston is to be used again be careful not to scratch it, and always use new circlips and small end bearings at the top end of the con-rod. Press out the gudgeon pin and carefully remove the piston. Special tools can be purchased, or a suitable sized socket used, to push the gudgeon pin through the piston.

Next, split the crankcase so that the crankshaft assembly can be removed, in preparation for splitting the crank in two to replace the con-rod and big end bearing. Press out and replace the main bearings and oil seals in the crank halves. If the crank halves are heated gently, the bearings will be more easily pressed out. The new bearings should be cold, and the crank halves warmed up so that they almost just drop into their seats.

A special press is needed to split the crankshaft to replace the big end bearing and con-rod.

From now on, access to specialist equipment and a degree of expertise is required, so it is best to take the crankshaft assembly and cylinder to a kart engine specialist. They will be able to split the crank shaft with a press, replace the big end bearing and con-rod, press them back together and true up the crank. They will also be able to hone or re-bore the cylinder if it has an iron liner.

It is very important to have honing or reboring carried out professionally, because if the cylinder is not left exactly parallel, excessive wear and damage can occur. Honing puts a fine criss-cross of marks on the cylinder wall, in order to retain the oil film for lubrication of the piston. If undamaged, cylinders with nikasil liners need little maintenance, other than cleaning the exhaust ports. The specialist will be able to measure the diameter of the liner properly, and advise on the correct size of replacement piston.

Reassembling the Engine

Reassembly is the reverse of stripping down. Ensure the bearings, big and small ends, cylinder liner and piston are all smeared with engine oil for initial lubrication, as well as the lips on the crankshaft seals. Use new gaskets, or possibly in the case of the crankshaft halves, a special silicon gasket cement. Before fitting a new piston ring, insert it into the top of the cylinder on top of a piston to square it up, and check the gap; if it is too small, it can be dressed off with a carborundum stone or small file. Ensure that all the nuts and bolts are tightened to the recommended torque values.

ESSENTIAL CHECKS TO THE REASSEMBLED ENGINE

After the engine has been assembled, certain measurements need to be taken to ensure correct operation. Depending on the type of engine, these include ignition timing, port timing, squish and head volume. The parameters for these measurements can be found in the engine instruction manuals, or by asking an engine expert. Some of the parameters may have limits which are not to be exceeded, otherwise the engine may be rejected when scrutineered after a race.

Ignition Timing

Briefly a dial gauge is inserted into the spark plug hole, using a special holder, and the engine rotated so the piston is at top dead centre. The gauge is set to zero, then the engine rotated backwards past the ignition point, which is normally marked with a line and set of marks on the stator and coil assembly. The crankshaft is now rotated in the direction that the engine normally runs until the marks align at the desired point, and the reading on the dial gauge read. This reading is a number of millimetres or thousands of an inch before top dead centre. The ignition is rotated until the desired reading is obtained.

Ignition timing is carried out with a dial gauge measuring piston height, against the marks on the rotor and stator.

Port Timing

To measure port timing a degree wheel or digital degree wheel is required. The analogue degree wheel is simply a 360 degree protractor, bolted to the end of the crankshaft. The more accurate digital version has a coder which fits onto the crankshaft, then connects to an electronic read-out. In both cases, after zeroing the wheel, the crankshaft is rotated in the desired direction with a thin feeler gauge inserted in the port until the rotation is stopped, and the reading taken. Port timing can be minimally adjusted by varying the thickness of the base gasket but this also affects head volume and squish.

Squish

The squish is the dimension between the outer edge of the piston and the cylinder head. It is measured by inserting a hooked piece of soft solder through the spark plug hole, ensuring it meets the edge of the cylinder wall. The engine is then smartly rotated so that the piston crimps the end of the piece of solder. The solder is then withdrawn and the thickness of the solder measured with a micrometer. It may be adjusted by changing the thickness or number of base gaskets at the cylinder and crankcase interface.

Head Volume

Class regulations often specify a minimum head volume. This is done to prevent the engines being tuned to the limit, thus in theory prolonging life and reducing costs. The head volume is checked by pouring a mixture of 50 per cent oil and 50 per cent petrol into the spark plug hole with the piston at top dead centre.

Ensure the engine is cool and at room temperature. Replace the spark plug with a special insert. Remove the cylinder head and put a thin smear of grease round the top of the cylinder, so that when the piston is turned to top dead centre it is sealed by the grease to prevent the fuel/oil mixture running down the side of the piston. Wipe off any excess grease. Taking care not to move the piston, refit the head, tightening the nuts to the correct torque setting. Ensure the top of the cylinder is exactly horizontal, using a spirit level.

Using a burette or pipette that can hold enough of the mixture, slowly drip it into the cylinder through the spark plug hole insert, until the fluid comes just level across the

Note the special insert in the spark plug hole, with the piston at TDC; the oil is measured in until it is level with the top of the insert.

top of the hole; then take the reading of the amount of mixture used. This is the volume of the cylinder head. With some engines the volume is quickly checked without needing to grease the top of the piston.

Once complete, or before trying again, the fluid must be tipped out, safely disposed of, and the head removed to wipe off any remaining drops before starting again. Specialist engine rebuilding companies and scrutineers may use a digital burette, which is very accurate, so an allowance should be made when using a normal burette not to be too near the limit. The insert generally uses 2ml, so the actual head volume will be 2ml less when measured in this way.

Gearbox engines

Engines with gears are more complicated, so very careful note should be taken of the fitment of the various gears and gear shift mechanisms when dismantling. Before taking the engine apart, and after draining the gearbox oil, it is worth swilling some petrol into the gearbox to wash off the oil and wash out any remaining swarf. It can then be drained through the drain plug. There will be a many bearings in the gearbox to check and replace if in any doubt. Carefully check all the teeth on the various gears for excessive wear or chips. Replace the oil seals, and when reassembled, refill the gearbox with the specified oil and correct volume.

Carburettor Checks and Maintenance

Carburettor adjustments are covered in Chapter 4. Diaphragm carburettors should have a rebuild after about every five hours of use. Kits containing replacement diaphragms and new gaskets are available. Float chamber carburettors should be stripped down and cleaned occasionally. The cut-off valve that opens to let fuel into the carburettor will probably need to be changed occasionally, and if there is a gauze filter fitted it will need to be cleaned or replaced occasionally. Having the correct height for the floats is very important: take advice from an engine tuner.

RUNNING IN

An engine needs a period of running in to bed in new components after a major rebuild. This is primarily for the piston to cylinder liner interface, as modern bearings

Gears should be inspected for wear.

This piston is showing excessive wear at one part.

require very little bedding in. The kart should be prepared with perhaps a couple of teeth fewer on the rear sprocket than normal, so that the engine cannot be over-revved, and the mixture set slightly richer than normal. Use bursts of full throttle, but initially do not allow the engine to reach full rpm. Slightly choke the engine each time the throttle is released, and build up gradually.

If the engine is not sealed and it is possible to remove the cylinder, the piston can be inspected to ensure it is bedding in properly with no shiny streaks down the piston surface which might indicate it is too

tight and needs more running-in time. Pistons that are coated with, for instance, a thin layer of Teflon and/ or running in a Nikasil coated liner need very little running in compared with a plain aluminium non-coated piston running in an iron liner – perhaps only five to ten minutes. Check with the engine manufacturer for the recommended running-in times.

Strangely enough the Comer W.60 Cadet engine needs no running in at all. For best ultimate performance it can be blasted up to full rpm almost immediately once warmed up.

Appendices

Appendix I: Summary of Main Kart Classes

Class	Number Plate/No.	Ages	Comments
			N.B. *TAG = 'Touch and go' – electric button start using an on-board battery.*
Comer Cadet	Yellow/black	8–13	60cc Comer sealed engine, clutch, pull starter
Honda Cadet	Yellow/red	8–13	GX160 four-stroke budget engine, clutch, pull starter
Cadet 2013	Yellow/black	8–13	New MSA contract for main Cadet engine commences 2013
Super Cadet	White/black	10–14	60cc homologated air-cooled engines, clutch, TAG unsealed
Junior TKM 2-Stroke	Blue/white	11–17	100cc air-cooled BT82 with choice of weight and restrictor, optional clutch, optional TAG
MiniMax	Yellow/black	11–15	Restricted version of Rotax Junior Max
Junior Max	Red/white	13–17	Junior version of Rotax Senior Max, 125cc water-cooled TAG with sealed engines
Formula Junior Blue	White/black	13–17	A 100cc TAG engine with different restrictors for different driver weights
KF3	Yellow/black	13–17	125cc International TAG class
TKM Extreme two-stroke	Red/white	16	115cc BT82, optional clutch, optional TAG
Rotax Max	Blue/white	16	125cc water-cooled TAG class with sealed engine
Rotax Max/177	Green/white	16	Heavyweight version of Rotax Max with 85kg min. driver weight
Formula Blue	Blue/white	16	A 100cc and 115cc TAG engine with a range of restrictors
KGP	Yellow/black	16	A 125cc TAG unsealed engine
KF2	White/black	16	International 125cc TAG class
KZ2 UK	Green/white	16	125cc reed-valve water-cooled engine with six gears and 30mm carburettor
250 National	White/black	16	Motocross 250cc single-cylinder engines (some clubs permit 450cc four-stroke karts)
Superkarts	Varies	16	Twin-cylinder 250cc engines
Formula 210	Red/white	16	Classic Villiers 197 or replica engines

Appendix II: Kart Clubs

Club/Circuit	Location	Usual race day	Website	Circuit telephone
Bayford Meadow	Eurolink Ind. Estate 1 mile east of Sittingbourne: ME10 3RY	4th Sunday	www.bayfordkarting.co.uk	01795 410707
Beccles/Ellough	2 miles from Beccles in Suffolk	Last Sunday	www.beccleskartclub.co.uk	01502 717718
Buckmore Park	Chatham, Kent between M2 J3 and M20 J6: ME5 9QG	3rd Sunday	www.buckmore.co.uk	0845 6037964
Camberley/ Blackbushe	Airfield off A30 near Yateley, Surrey	4th Saturday	www.camberleykartclub.com	N/A
Cheshire/ Hooton Park	Near Ellesmere Port	2nd Sunday	www.chkrc.co.uk	N/A
Clay Pigeon	Mid-way Yeovil/ Dorchester on the A37	2nd Sunday	www.claypigeonkartclub.com	01935 83713
Cumbria/Rowrah	4 miles from Frizington, Cumbria	2nd Sunday	www.cumbriakrc.co.uk	N/A
Dragon Kart Club/ Glan-y-Gors Park	Conwy, 10 miles from Corwn, off A5 North Wales	3rd Sunday	www.dragonkartclub.com	01490 420770
Dunkeswell/ Mansell Raceway	5 miles from Honiton, Devon	Last Sunday	www.dunkeswellkartclub.co.uk	N/A
East Scotland/Crail	Fife, NO 627 094	Varies	www.eskc.net	N/A
Forest Edge	Barton Stacey near Andover, off A303	1st Sunday	www.fekc.co.uk	N/A
Grampian/Boyndie	3 miles west of Banff, Banffshire	2nd Sunday	www.grampiankartclub.com	N/A
Guernsey/ St Sampsons	Guernsey, Channel Islands	Varies	www.gmccc.co.uk	N/A
Hoddesdon/ Rye House	Rye Road, Hoddesdon: EN11 0EH	1st Sunday	www.hoddesdonkartclub.co.uk	01992 460895
Hunts/ Kimbolton	10 miles WSW of Huntingdon, north of village	2nd Sunday	www.hkrc.co.uk	N/A
Isle of Man/Jurby	Near Douglas, Isle of Man	Varies	www.iomkra.com	N/A
Jersey/Sorel Point	Sorel Point, St John, Jersey	Varies	jerseykartclub.com	N/A
Kent/Lydd	Dengemarsh Rd South of Lydd Kent	Varies	www.lyddkarting.com	01797 321747
Lincs/Fulbeck	Stragglethorpe, Newark, between A17 and A1	4th Sunday	www.lkrc.uk.com	N/A
Llandow	9 miles from Cardiff on B4270	2nd Sunday	www.llandowkartclub.co.uk	01446 795568

Appendix II: Kart Clubs *(continued...)*

Club/Circuit	Location	Usual race day	Website	Circuit telephone
Manchester & Buxton/ Three Sisters	Bryn Road, Ashton-in-Makerfield near Wigan	4th Sunday	www.mbkartclub.com	01942 270230
NATSKA/Varies	Varies	Varies	www.natska.co.uk	N/A
North of Scotland/ Golspie	Little Ferry, Golspie, Sutherland	Last Sunday	www.nskc.co.uk	N/A
RAF MSA/Varies	N/A	Varies	www.raf.mod.uk/rafmotor-sports/4wheels/rafkarting.cfm	N/A
Rissington	Ex-RAF airfield, Little Rissington, Stow, Glos.	1st Sunday	www.rissykartclub.com	N/A
Shenington/Shenington Airfield	8 miles NW Banbury, Oxon, off A422: OX15 6NW	3rd Sunday	www.sheningtonkrc.co.uk	01295 688035
Stars/Varies	Varies	Varies	www.formulakartstars.com	N/A
South Yorks/ Wombwell	Wombwell Sports Stadium, 6 miles Barnsley	2nd Sunday Varies	www.southyorkshirekart-club.co.uk	N/A
Trent Valley/ PF International	1 mile from Brandon, Newark between the A17 and A1	1st Sunday	tvkc.co.uk	01636 626424
Ulster/ Nutts Corner	4 miles from Crumlin, Northern Ireland	Varies	www.ulsterkartingclub.co.uk	02890 825301
West of Scotland/ Larkhall	South of Hamilton Strathclyde, off M74	3rd Sunday Varies	www.wskc.co.uk	N/A
Whilton Mill	5 miles east of Daventry East from A5 junction	4th Sunday/ Varies	www.whiltonmillkartclub.co.uk	01327 843822

Appendix III: ARKS Schools

Please visit www.arks.co.uk for the latest information and list of currently approved professional schools.

Bayford Meadows Kart School
Bayford Meadows Kart School,
Bayford Meadows Kart Circuit,
Symmonds Drive, Eurolink Industrial Estate, Sittingbourne, Kent ME10 3RY
Tel: 01795 410707
Fax: 01795 423814
Email: info@bmkr.co.uk
Web: www.bayfordkarting.co.uk

DRIVE-TECH Ltd
Castle Combe Circuit, Chippenham, Wilts SN14 7BW
Tel: 01249 783010
Fax: 01249 783223
Email: info@drivetechltd.co.uk
Web: www.drivetechltd.co.uk

Nutts Corner ARKS School
Nutts Corner Motorsport Centre, 11 Dundrod Road, Nutts Corner, Crumlin BT29 4SR
Tel: 02890 825301 Mobile 07850 969744
Fax: 02890812144
Email: info@nuttscornercircuit.com
Web: www.nuttscornercircuit.com

Lee Rennison Kart Racing School
Clay Pigeon Raceway, Wardon Hill, nr Dorchester DT2 9PW
Tel: 01935 83713
Fax: 01935 83792
Email: ianrennison@btconnect.com
www.claypigeonraceway.com

Superkarting-UK Racing Kart Club School
Secretary, 157 Carlton Avenue, Tunstall, Stoke-on-Trent, Staffs ST6 7HF
Tel: 01782 826111 Mob: 07831 854896
Web: www.superkarting-uk.com

Motorsport World ARKS Academy
Rye House Stadium, Rye Road,
Hoddesdon, Herts EN11 0EH
Tel: 01992 460895
Fax: 01992 468812
Web: www.rye-house.co.uk

Protrain Karting Courses
Protrain Karting Courses Unit 6,
Hillcrest Way Buckingham Industrial
Park, Buckingham MK18 1HJ
Tel: 01280 814774
Fax: 01280 814007
Email: protrain@karttraining.co.uk
Web: www.karttraining.co.uk

Sisley Racing School
Buckmore Park Kart Circuit,
Maidstone Road, Chatham, Kent ME5
9QG
Tel: 01634 201562
Fax: 01634 686104
Email: sales@buckmore.co.uk
Web: www.buckmore.co.uk

The Racing School
Three Sisters Race Circuit, Byrn
Road, Ashton-in-Makerfield, Nr
Wigan, Lancs WN4 8DD
Tel: 01942 270230
Fax: 01942 270508
Email: sales@racing-school.co.uk
Web: www.aintree-racing-drivers-
school.co.uk

Thruxton Motorsport Centre
Thruxton Circuit, Andover, Hampshire
SP11 8PW
Tel: 01264 882222 / 01264 882231
Fax: 01264 882201
Email: jennie@thruxtonracing.co.uk
Web: www.thruxtonkarting.co.uk

Tockwith Motorsports
Control Tower Office, Tockwith
Airfield, Tockwith near York YO26
7QF
Tel: 01423 358501
Fax: 01423 358865
Email:
simon@tockwithmotorsports.net
Web: www.tockwithmotorsports.net

Cambuslang Karting
91 Glasgow Road, Cambuslang,
Glasgow G72 7BT
Tel: 0141 641 0921
Mob: 07984 807 183
Email: iain@cambuslangkarting.com
Web: www.cambuslangkarting.com

Ziemelis Motorsport, Podium
House, 10 The Highway, Great
Staughton, Huntingdon, Cams PE19
4DA
Tel: 01295 760091 / 07860 742386
Fax: 01480 861297
Email:
Stuart@ziemelismotorsport.com
Web: www.ziemelismotorsport.com

Appendix IV: Organizations and Useful Websites

Motor Sports Association (MSA)
Motor Sports House, Riverside Park,
Colnbrook SL3 0HG
Tel: 01753 765000 Licence inquiries:
01753 765050
Fax: 01753 682938
Web: www.msauk.org

Governing body for four-wheeled
motor sport in the UK.

**Commission Internationale de
Karting-FIA (CIK)**
2 Chemin de Blandonnet, 1215
Geneva15, Switzerland
Tel: +41 22 306 10 80
Fax: +41 22 306 10 90
Web: www.cikfia.com

International governing body for kart
racing.

**Association of British Kart Clubs
(ABkC)**
Stoneycroft, Godsons Lane, Napton,
Southam CV47 8LX

Tel: 01926 812177
Web: www.abkc.org.uk

Nearly all the kart clubs in the UK are
members of the ABKC.

**Association of Racing Kart
Schools (ARKS)**
Stoneycroft, Godsons Lane, Napton,
Southam CV47 8LX
Tel: 01926 812177
Web: www.arks.co.uk

The professional MSA-approved kart
schools.

British Kart Industry Association (BKIA)
PO Box 2122, Worthing BN12 9DA
Tel: 01903 241921
Web: www.bkia.co.uk

The body which represents the teams, kart traders and manufacturers in the UK.

Super One Series (S1)
Manley House Farm, Manley Lane, Manley, Cheshire WA6 0PF
Tel: 07774 646784
Web: www.s1series.co.uk

The UK's premier kart series, holds British and National championships.

Formula Kart Stars (FKS)
Snowball Farm, Westbury, Brackley, Northamptonshire NN13 5JP
Tel: 07973 55317
Web: www.formulakartstars.com

A multi-class series which includes the British Cadet championship.

Karting **Magazine**
Lodgemark Press, Moorfield House, 15 Moorfield Road, Orpington, Kent BR6 0XD
Tel: 01689 897123
Web: www.kartingmagazine.com

Monthly magazine (print and on-line), and also stockists of a large range of books and DVDs.

Long circuit racing
www.superkart.org.uk/

Web site for the long circuit racing championships.

British Historic Kart Club
www.britishhistorickartclub.com/

The club for classic and historic kart owners and enthusiasts.

Appendix V: Kart Circuits

Circuit	Location	Website	Circuit Telephone
Bayford Meadow	Eurolink Industrial Estate, 1 mile east of Sittingbourne: ME10 3RY	www.bayfordkarting.co.uk	01795 410707
Blackbushe	Airfield off A30 near Yateley, Surrey	www.camberleykartclub.com	N/A
Boyndie	3 miles west of Banff, Banffshire	www.grampiankartclub.com	N/A
Buckmore Park	Chatham, Kent between M2 J3 and M20 J6: ME5 9QG	www.buckmore.co.uk	0845 6037964
Clay Pigeon	Mid-way Yeovil/ Dorchester on A37	www.claypigeonraceway.com	01935 83713
Ellough Park	2 miles from Beccles in Suffolk	www.elloughparkraceway.co.uk	01502 717718
Forest Edge	Barton Stacey, near Andover, off A303	www.fekc.co.uk	
Fulbeck	Stragglethorpe, Newark, between A17 and A1	www.lkrc.uk.com	
Glan-y-Gors Park	Conwy 10 miles from Corwn, off A5 North Wales	www.gygkarting.co.uk	01490 420770
Golspie	Little Ferry, Golspie, Sutherland	www.nskc.co.uk	
Hooton Park	Near Ellesmere Port	www.chkrc.co.uk	
Jurby	Near Douglas, Isle of Man	www.iomkra.com	
Kimbolton	10 miles WSW of Huntingdon, north of village	www.hkrc.co.uk	
Larkhall	South of Hamilton, Strathclyde, off M74	www.wskc.co.uk	
Llandow	9 miles from Cardiff, on B4270	www.swkc.co.uk	01446 795568
Mansell Raceway	5 miles from Honiton, Devon	www.mansellraceway.com	0844 544 1992
Nutts Corner	4 miles from Crumlin, Northern Ireland	www.nuttscornercircuit.com	02890 825301
PF International	1 mile from Brandon, Newark between A17 and A1	www.jmkartsport.co.uk	01636 626424
Rissington	Ex-RAF airfield, Little Rissington, Stow, Glos	www.rissykartclub.com	
Rowrah	4 miles from Frizington, Cumbria	www.cumbriakrc.co.uk	

Kart Circuits *(continued...)*

Rye House	Rye Road, Hoddesdon EN11 0EH	www.rye-house.co.uk	01992 460895
Shenington Airfield	8 miles NW Banbury, Oxon, off A422: OX15 6NW	www.sheningtonkrc.co.uk	01295 688035
St Sampsons	Guernsey, Channel Islands	www.gmccc.co.uk	
Three Sisters	Bryn Road, Ashton-in-Makerfield, near Wigan	www.three-sisters.co.uk	01942 270230
Whilton Mill	5 miles east of Daventry, east from A5 junction	www.whiltonmill.co.uk	01327 843822
Wombwell	Wombwell Sports Stadium, 6 miles Barnsley	www.southyorkshirekart-club.co.uk	
Crail	Former airfield near Crail, in Fife	www.eskc.net	
Lydd	Dengemarsh Road, south of Lydd, Kent	www.lyddkarting.com	01797 321747
Sorel Point	Sorel Point, St John, Jersey	jerseykartclub.com	

Index